AF594802

CONSTABLE

CONSTABLE

Tim Barringer

with an essay by

Nicholas Robbins

YALE CENTER FOR BRITISH ART

Distributed by Yale University Press
New Haven and London

Produced by the Department of Publications
Yale Center for British Art
Don McMahon, Head of Publications
Julie Fry, Head of Design
Miciah Hussey, Publications Manager
Victoria Hepburn, Project Specialist
Rhyannon van Alstyne, Publications Assistant

Design and production by Julie Fry
Edited by Sarah Resnick
Proofread by Claire Lehmann
Indexed by Kathleen Friello
Image research by Cristyn Filla
Printed and bound by Graphius, Ghent

Typeset in Caslon and Freight
Printed on GardaPat Kiara

Published by the Yale Center for British Art
britishart.yale.edu

ISBN: 978-0-300-28466-9
Library of Congress Control Number: 2025934428

All images courtesy Yale Center for British Art except p. 11, fig. 2: National Portrait Gallery, London; p. 12, fig. 3, British Museum, London; p. 13, fig. 4: National Gallery, London; p. 13, fig. 5: © Peter Kennard, courtesy of Tate Britain, London; p. 16, fig. 7: Yale University Art Gallery; p. 16, fig. 8: National Gallery, London; p. 22, fig. 11: Museum of Fine Arts, Boston; p. 21, fig. 12: The Clark Art Institute, Williamstown, Massachusetts; p. 23, fig. 14: National Gallery, London; p. 23, fig. 14: Private Collection; p. 26, fig. 16: Tate Britain, London; p. 27, fig. 17: Fuji Museum, Tokyo; p. 29, fig. 18: Tate Britain, London; p. 31, fig. 21: Tate Britain, London; p. 34, fig. 23: Yale University Art Gallery; p. 111, fig. 4: Yale University, Beinecke Rare Book and Manuscript Library; p. 117, fig. 13: Yale University, Beinecke Rare Book and Manuscript Library; p. 117, fig. 14: Whitworth Art Gallery, University of Manchester.

Distributed by Yale University Press
New Haven and London
yalebooks.com | yalebooks.co.uk

Jacket illustrations
Front: John Constable, *Hadleigh Castle, The Mouth of the Thames—Morning after a Stormy Night*, 1829 (detail of plate 38)
Back: John Constable, *Golding Constable's House, East Bergholt: The Artist's Birthplace*, ca. 1809 (plate 6)

Printed and bound in Belgium

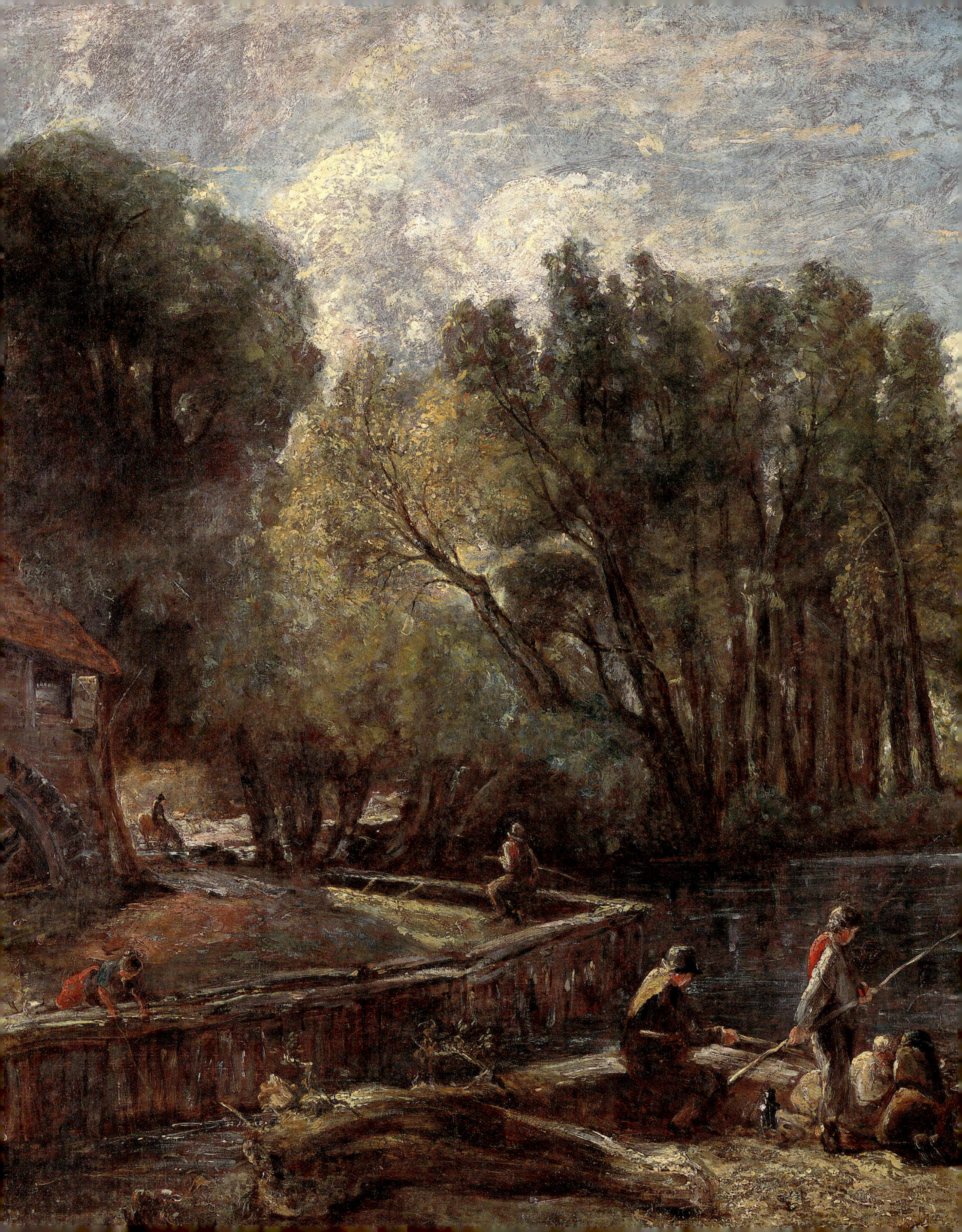

FOREWORD

If one word could be chosen to characterize John Constable, it might be "contradictory." In his most ambitious works, he expanded the scale of landscape art to compete with the grandeur of history painting. Yet most of his monumental works depict a tiny corner of the world—his beloved "own places" along the River Stour in Suffolk. Indeed, today no other artist is as deeply associated with the English countryside. But, surprisingly, in his lifetime and immediately after his death, he was more influential in France than in England. By the end of the nineteenth century, art lovers from further afield, including in the United States, had taken to his art.

Paul Mellon, who founded the Yale Center for British Art, followed in the footsteps of earlier American collectors. By the time he exhibited his Constables in 1969 at the National Gallery in Washington, DC, he had developed so comprehensive a collection that it was billed as providing a full account of the artist's career. Thanks to his founding bequest, we have continued to acquire works that provide insight into Constable's deeply innovative practices: *Stratford Mill* (plate 17) exemplifies the full-scale sketches the artist produced for the colossal "six-footers" he exhibited at the Royal Academy in London. The more recent acquisition of a smaller painting, *Hampstead Heath* (plate 24), adds to our knowledge of the studies he produced *en plein air*—a body of work that includes his transcriptions of levitating clouds, explored here in an essay by Nicholas Robbins.

As Tim Barringer deftly illuminates in this volume, although Constable's landscapes are often profoundly personal, they also grapple with questions about the rapidly changing world around him. His compositions offer not only an idyll to contrast with the social transformations he—a staunch traditionalist—found so unsettling, but also a rural counterpoint to unbridled industrialization, whose damaging effects on the environment they seem so presciently to protest.

Martina Droth, Paul Mellon Director

Full-Size Sketch for "Stratford Mill" 1819–20 (detail of plate 17)

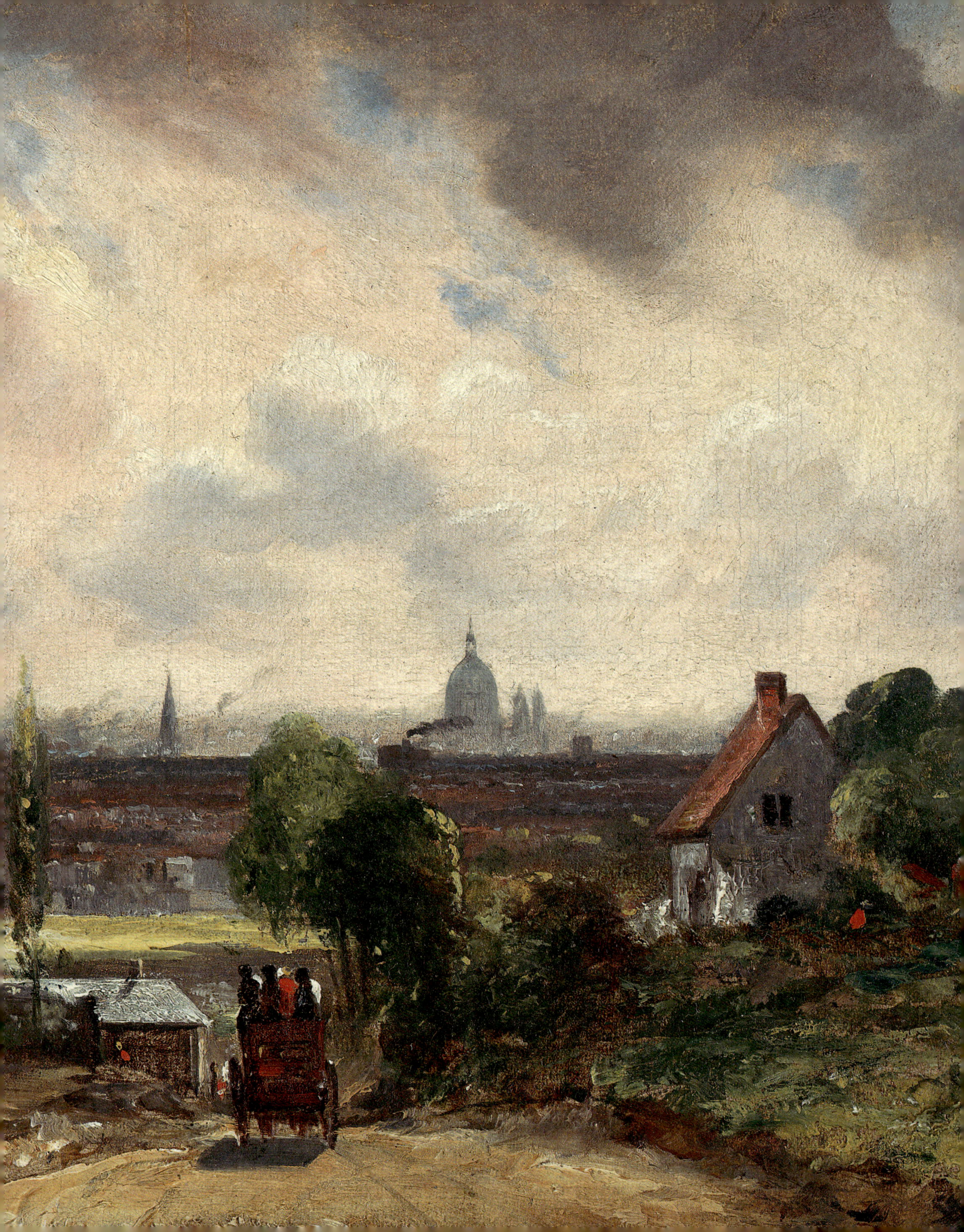

Mr. Constable's English Landscape

Tim Barringer

Summing up his life's work in 1831, John Constable (1776–1837) assembled a series of paintings and drawings for publication. The engraver David Lucas (1802–1881) was to reproduce them in mezzotint, a method of printmaking whose intense tonal contrasts might capture the visual drama of Constable's art. The paintings Constable selected for the series, known as *English Landscape*, were notable for the swift movement of the painter's brush, tracking the play of light and shade as sunshine followed showers; they captured, in his own words, the "chiar'oscuro of nature."

Beneath the inscription "Frontispiece to Mr. Constable's English Landscape," we find a modest image titled *East Bergholt, Suffolk* (fig. 1). Amid mature trees, against a stormy sky filled with crows in flight, sits a stately brick farmhouse. Sturdily built, its large, elegant windows suggest rooms for genteel entertainment. This is East Bergholt House, where John Constable was born on June 11, 1776. A man seated on the ground, in the lower-right corner, sketches, his dog by his side. Surely this is a surrogate for Constable himself: an eyewitness, a faithful observer of nature's moods. At the foot of the page, Constable quotes a Latin poem, which his friend the Reverend John Fisher (1788–1832) translated as

This spot saw the day-spring of my Life,
Hours of Joy, and years of Happiness;
This place first tinged my boyish fancy with a love of the Art,
This place was the origin of my fame.

Sir Richard Steele's Cottage, Hampstead 1831–32 (detail of plate 35)

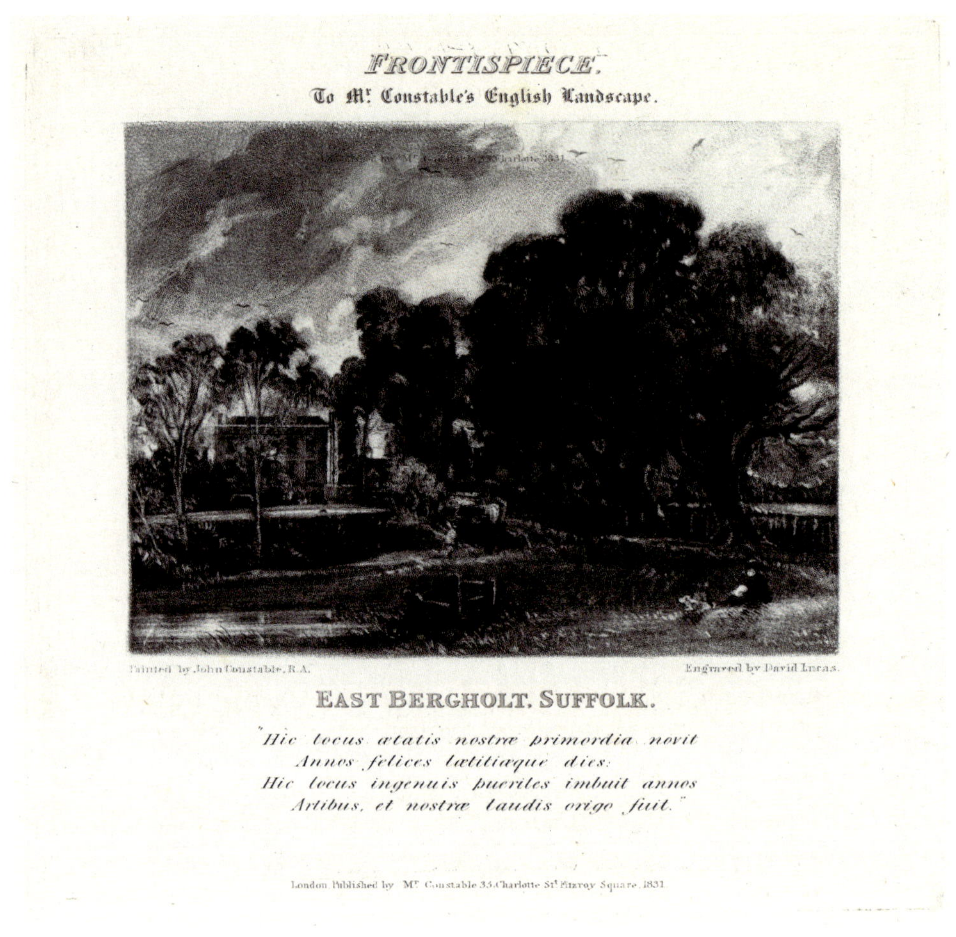

FIG. 1 David Lucas (English, 1802–1881) after John Constable (English, 1776–1837), *Frontispiece, Artist's Home at East Bergholt, Suffolk* (from *English Landscape*), 1831, mezzotint, 11¾ × 17½ in. (29.8 × 44.5 cm)

Professional and personal demands drew Constable to London, center of the art world, for much of his life; but East Bergholt and the surrounding countryside remained foremost in his imagination. The village lies in Suffolk, a verdant agricultural county in the east of England where Constable's father, Golding, a prosperous merchant, owned a flour mill and several river barges. This comfortable family background gave Constable a distinctive position in the elaborate social hierarchy of the age whose nuances are deftly explored in the novels of Jane Austen, born the year before the painter. Although not a member of the hereditary landed classes, Constable was a young gentleman of means. So he appears in an early self-portrait elegantly attired, with a hint of foppishness in the combing

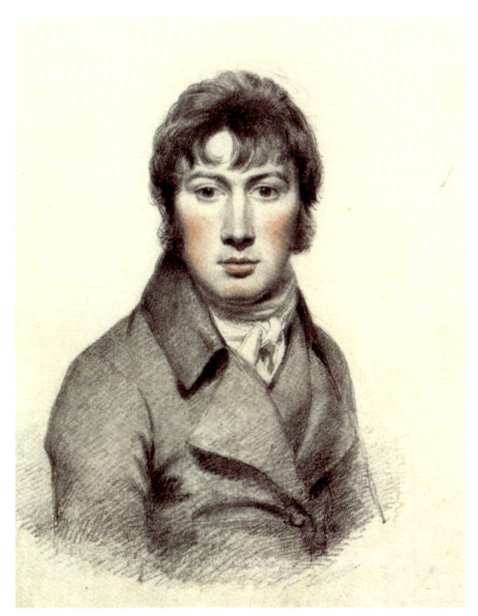

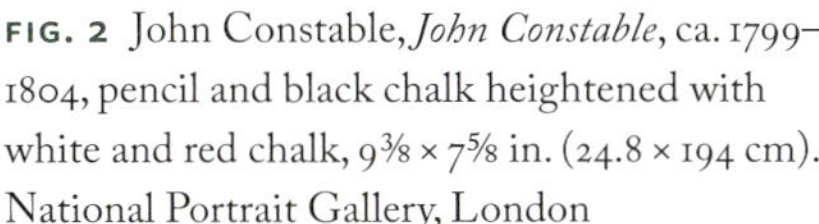

FIG. 2 John Constable, *John Constable*, ca. 1799–1804, pencil and black chalk heightened with white and red chalk, 9⅜ × 7⅝ in. (24.8 × 194 cm). National Portrait Gallery, London

of his forelock (fig. 2). John's parents, imagining for their son a respectable future as a clergyman, resisted his ambition to become an artist, a profession on the fringes of respectability.

A countryman, Constable understood the daily life of a traditional rural community, the rhythms of the agricultural year, and the moods of the seasons. These themes percolate throughout his major works, underscored with a melancholy recognition that profound changes were underway, driven by industrialization, the growth of cities, and political reform. In 1829 his contemporary, the satirical draughtsman George Cruikshank, produced an etching subtitled *The March of Bricks and Mortar*. Serried ranks of building materials displace trees, haystacks, and livestock, typical subjects of Constable's art, who run for their lives (fig. 3). Painfully aware of the ecological as well as social changes of the era, Constable knew that the idyllic rural scenes he painted, always something of a fantasy, would soon be consigned to the past.

Although profoundly rooted in the local, his artistic project was national in ambition. Since his death in 1837, Constable's work has come to stand for England itself—a development he would perhaps have welcomed. Painted on a grand scale and first shown in 1821, his masterpiece, exhibited with the title *Landscape: Noon* and now known as *The Hay Wain*, has been on display at the National Gallery in London since 1886 (fig. 4). Acclaimed by critics and the

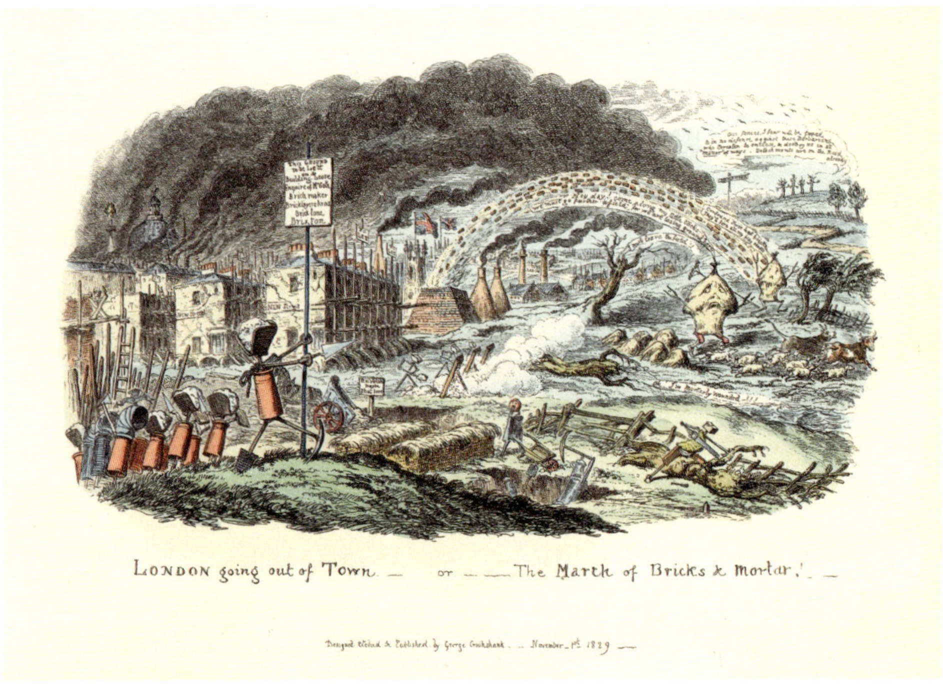

FIG. 3 George Cruikshank (English, 1792–1878), *London Going Out of Town—or—The March of Bricks and Mortar*, 1829, hand-colored etching, 7⅝ × 10⅜ in. (19.2 × 26.2 cm). British Museum, London

public alike, it has become an icon of national identity. Reproduced on postcards, tea towels, and calendars, and ubiquitous in digital form, *The Hay Wain* feeds the powerful myth that England, industrial and urban, remains an unchanging rural paradise. When the artist and activist Peter Kennard wanted to protest the positioning of US cruise missiles in Britain in 1980, he chose this most English of all images for a satirical collage (fig. 5).

The Hay Wain is no mere symbol of place or nation, however. A work of striking freshness and visual originality, it grew from a tiny study now at the Yale Center for British Art (plate 20). Painted with oils on a fragment of canvas measuring just less than five inches by seven, this sketch carries a dynamic visual charge. Working quickly, Constable blocked out the masses of the composition. He applied the paint thickly, energetic brushstrokes suggesting the fleeting effects of light as a summer storm passes over the nearby fields. The painting's narrative is simple: An empty cart, a hay wain, is stopped from crossing a ford after a sudden flood caused by a thunderstorm; later it will collect the hay being cut in the distance. The narrative belongs to a timeless pastoral realm.

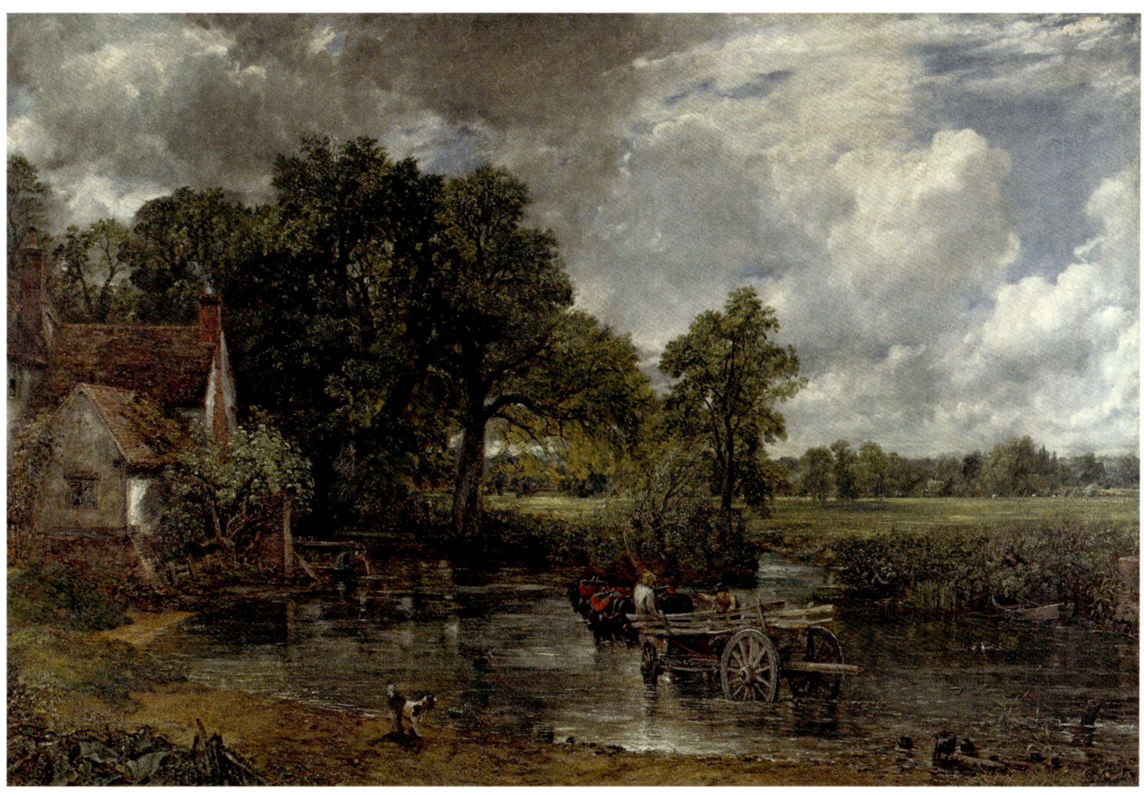

FIG. 4 John Constable, *The Hay Wain*, 1821, oil on canvas, 51¼ × 73 in. (130.2 × 185.4 cm). National Gallery, London

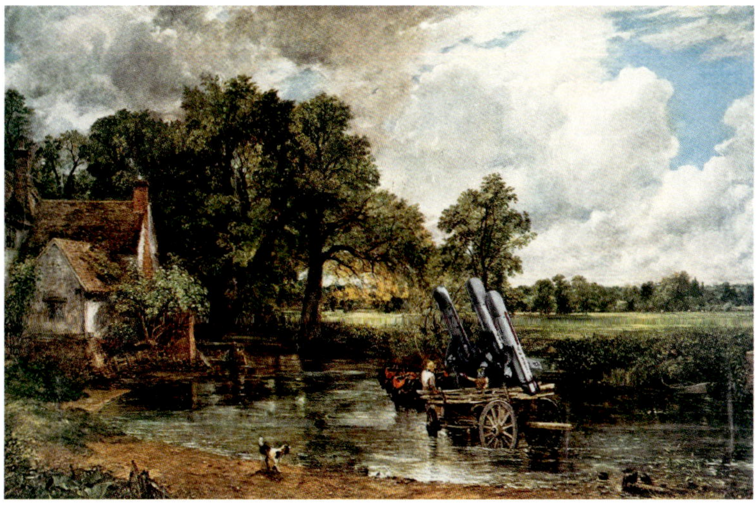

FIG. 5 Peter Kennard (English, b. 1949), *Haywain with Cruise Missiles*, 1980, chromo lithograph and photographs, 10¼ × 14¾ in. (26 × 37.5 cm). Tate Britain, London

But both sketch and exhibited canvas share an explosive level of visual energy, a sense of motion and immediacy that remains, after two centuries, vibrantly and emphatically modern.

"MY *OLD MEN*"

The annual juried exhibition at the Royal Academy of Arts was the most significant event in the London art world. Constable first exhibited in 1802, at twenty-five, the age at which his rival, J. M. W. Turner (1775–1851), had been elected an associate member of the Royal Academy, placing him among the artistic elite. Constable's route to his modest professional debut had been slow. After a period working for the family business, he entered the Royal Academy schools in 1799. There he strove to master figure drawing, first from plaster casts of classical sculpture and eventually from the nude model (plate 47).

Before this professional training began, Constable had found kindred spirits and mentors to support his artistic inclinations. One was the local handyman John Dunthorne (1770–1844), a colorful character who made musical instruments and painted inn signs. Self-taught as a landscape artist, Dunthorne took Constable sketching in the countryside, teaching him the rudiments. When the aspirant painter was dispatched to gain business experience in Edmonton, near London, he developed cordial relations with John Cranch (1751–1821), a learned eccentric. Cranch introduced Constable to the major texts of artistic theory and challenged his young protégé to master the "art of selecting and combining, from the whole, that which will best satisfy at once the eye."

Early drawings reveal that Constable had absorbed the fashionable conventions of the picturesque, an aesthetic theory rooted in a touristic enjoyment of landscape. It emphasized rough textures and favored irregular or ruinous structures, the artist often alighting on them from oblique angles. Constable would constantly return to picturesque subjects, from the ruins of St. Botolph's Priory, Colchester, in 1809 (fig. 6), to Hadleigh Castle, Essex, and Salisbury Cathedral, Wiltshire, later in his career.

During these early years, Constable acquired a thorough knowledge of the artistic canon. A mentor in this endeavor was the printmaker and antiquarian John Thomas Smith (1766–1833), who lent Constable old master etchings and engravings from his collection to study and copy. Later in life, Constable would form a substantial collection of his own, which acted as a visual reference library of fine art. Most significant were two thousand painters' etchings and a further thousand engravings after French, Flemish, and Dutch masters. These he affectionately called "my *old men*." Their echoes can be seen throughout his work.

While he admired British landscape painters of previous generations, particularly Richard Wilson (1713/14–1782) and Suffolk-born Thomas Gainsborough (1727–1788), the two artists whom Constable truly revered were Peter Paul Rubens (1577–1640) and Claude Lorrain (1604/5–1682). A family connection procured Constable an introduction to the connoisseur, collector, and amateur painter George Beaumont (1753–1827), whose mother lived at Dedham. Beaumont owned fine works by both seventeenth-century masters and took an interest in the enthusiastic autodidact, allowing him to make copies. Claude's pastoral landscapes are works of high artifice, drawing together elements of the

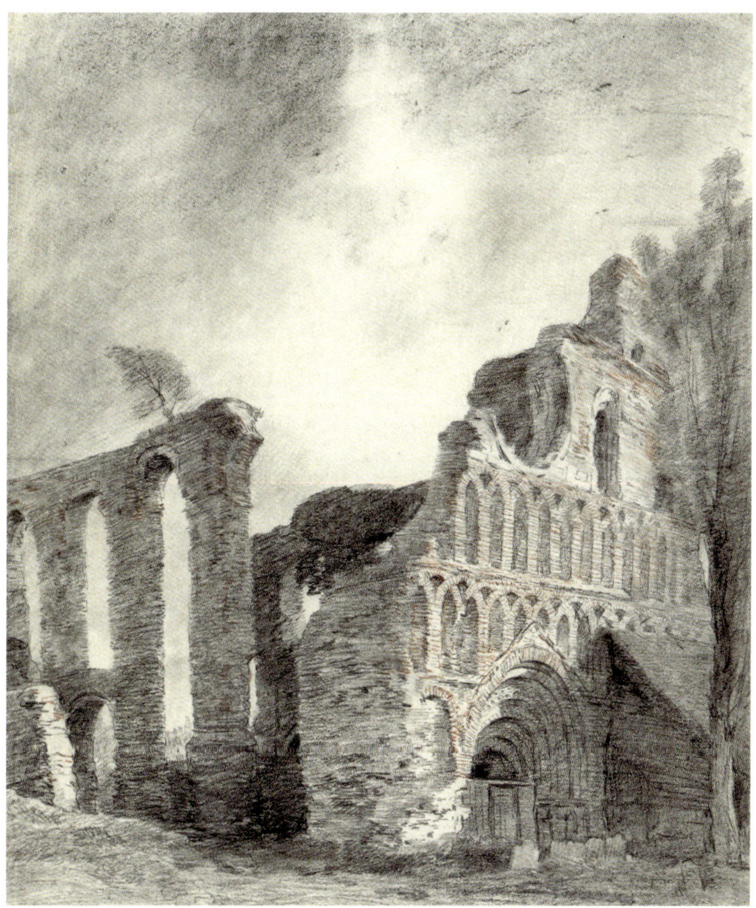

FIG. 6 John Constable, *Ruin of St. Botolph's Priory, Colchester*, ca. 1809, black chalk, brown chalk, and graphite, 17⅛ × 14⅞ in. (43.5 × 37.8 cm). Yale Center for British Art, Paul Mellon Collection

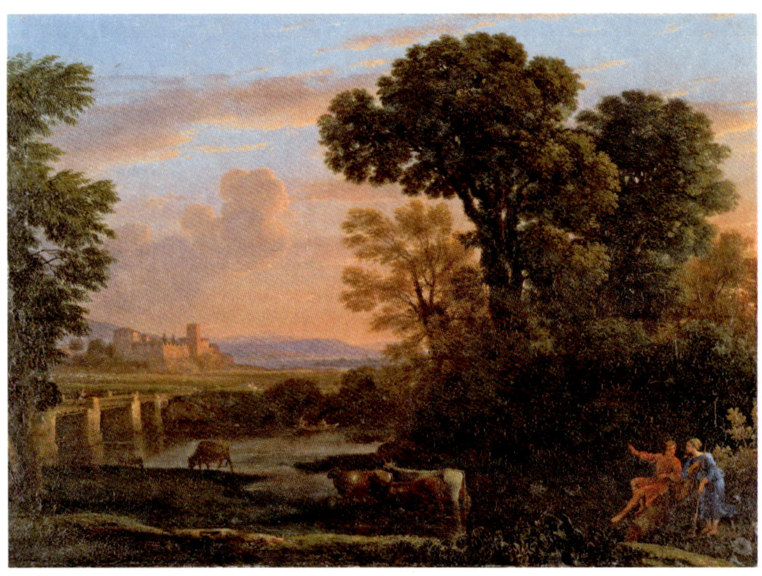

FIG. 7 Claude Lorrain (French, 1604/5–1682), *Pastoral Landscape*, 1648, oil on copper, 23¼ × 29 in. (59.1 × 73.7 cm). Yale University Art Gallery

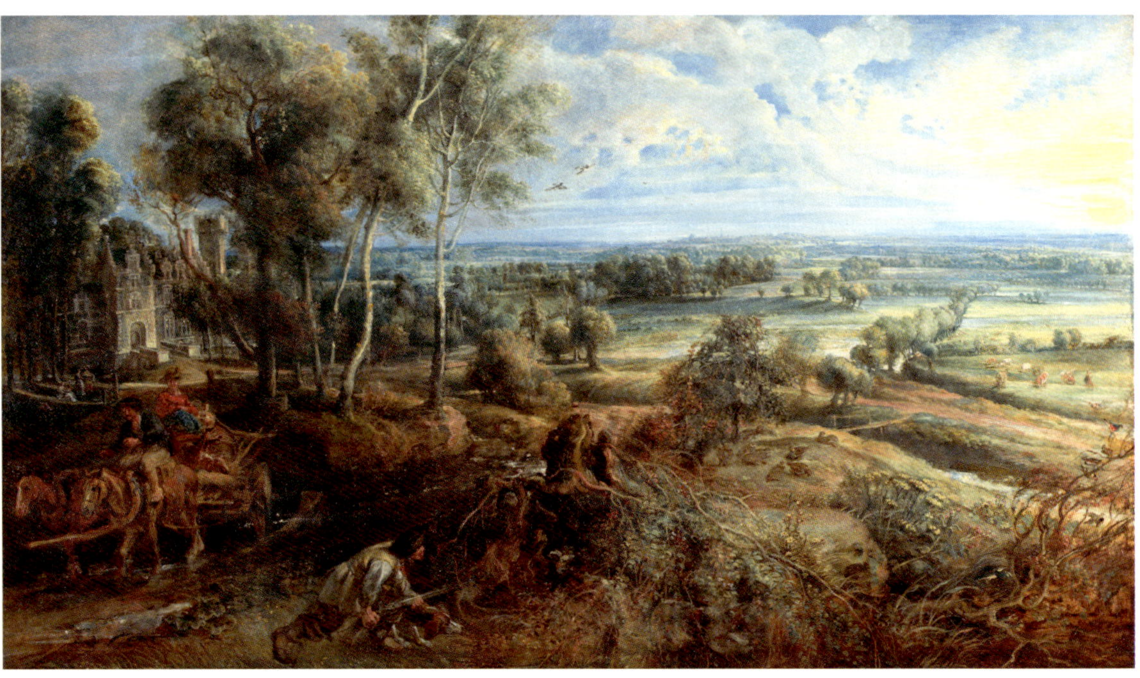

FIG. 8 Peter Paul Rubens (Flemish, 1577–1640), *An Autumn Landscape with a View of Het Steen in the Early Morning*, probably 1636, oil on wood, 51⅝ × 90¼ in. (131.2 × 229.2 cm). National Gallery, London

Campagna di Roma into elegant compositions framed by graceful trees; the eye is drawn through sunshine and shade, past a lake or river, to cool, blue mountains on the horizon (fig. 7). Collected by British aristocrats like Beaumont, who had traveled to Italy on the Grand Tour, Claude's compositions decisively influenced landscape garden design and shaped the work of painters such as Wilson. Constable, too, learned much from the French painter's mastery of form, but he rejected the weatherless stasis of Claude's arcadia and disavowed Beaumont's reactionary insistence that modern painters should merely replicate the formulae of their distinguished forebears. Another work in Beaumont's collection, *Autumn Landscape with a View of Het Steen in the Early Morning*, by Rubens, offered an alternative vision (fig. 8). Constable admired the "freshness and dewy light, the joyous and animated character which he has imparted to it, impressing on the level monotonous scenery of Flanders all the richness which belongs to its noblest features." Rubens, Constable added, "delighted in phenomena—rainbows upon a stormy sky—bursts of sunshine—moonlight—Meteors—and impetuous torrents." It was this northern European vision, presenting the real not the ideal, that the young Suffolk painter vowed to emulate, rather than the static Elysian Fields of Claude.

Constable spent time with Beaumont's paintings in May 1802, while his own work, still heavily influenced by Gainsborough, was on view at the Academy for the first time. At this time, he wrote a letter to Dunthorne that amounted to a manifesto: "For these two years past I have been running after pictures and seeking the truth at second hand," he began.

> *I shall shortly return to Bergholt where I shall make some laborious studies from nature—and I shall endeavour to get a pure and unaffected representation of the scenes that may employ me with respect to colour particularly. . . . There is little or nothing in the exhibition worth looking up to—there is room enough for a natural painture.*

PAINTING FROM NATURE

Back in Suffolk, Constable completed *Lane near Dedham* (fig. 9) and *Dedham Vale* (plate 1). At first glance these small works, relatively uniform in tone, appear modest and understated; close looking, however, reveals a multitude of observed detail and a refreshing sense of nature's exuberance. Painted on adjacent fragments of a larger canvas, they embody Constable's new naturalism, registering the distinctive appearance of every object, however mundane. Each tree has its

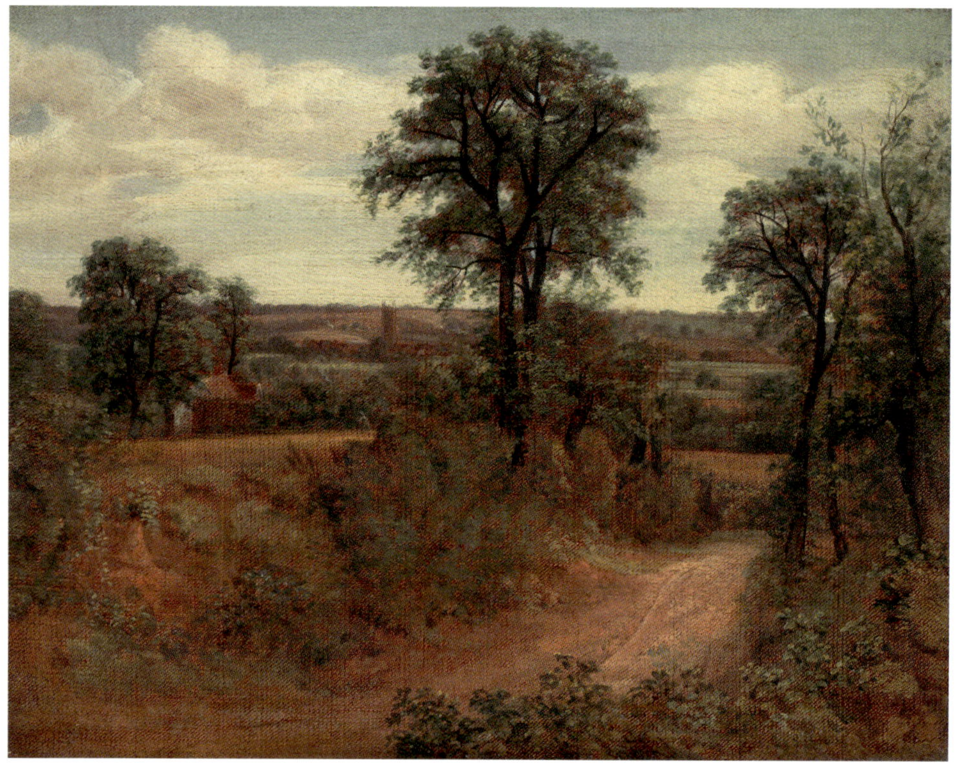

FIG. 9 John Constable, *Lane near Dedham*, 1802, oil on canvas, 13⅛ × 16¾ in. (33.3 × 42.5 cm). Yale Center for British Art, Paul Mellon Collection

own character, as if the subject of a portrait painting; the turf itself seems to find a material analogue in the sandy paint above the layer of brown underpaint with which the canvas had been prepared. A ghostly trace of Claude is still present in each, with a mass of framing trees (known as a *repoussoir*); patches of light and shade draw the viewer's eye toward a distant horizon. The Claudean model also shaped Constable's drawings of the period (plate 48). But we are in Suffolk, not Arcadia. Constable scrawled "Sep" on the stretcher of *Lane near Dedham*, and the picture exudes the fresh smell of standing wheat in the humid harvest air of September.

The first decade of the nineteenth century found Constable struggling to establish himself professionally. He took on commissions for portraits, some from well-to-do members of his extended family, such as Captain Richard Gubbins (plate 2). Trying his hand at other potentially lucrative genres, he visited country houses such as Malvern Hall, in Warwickshire, where in 1809 he

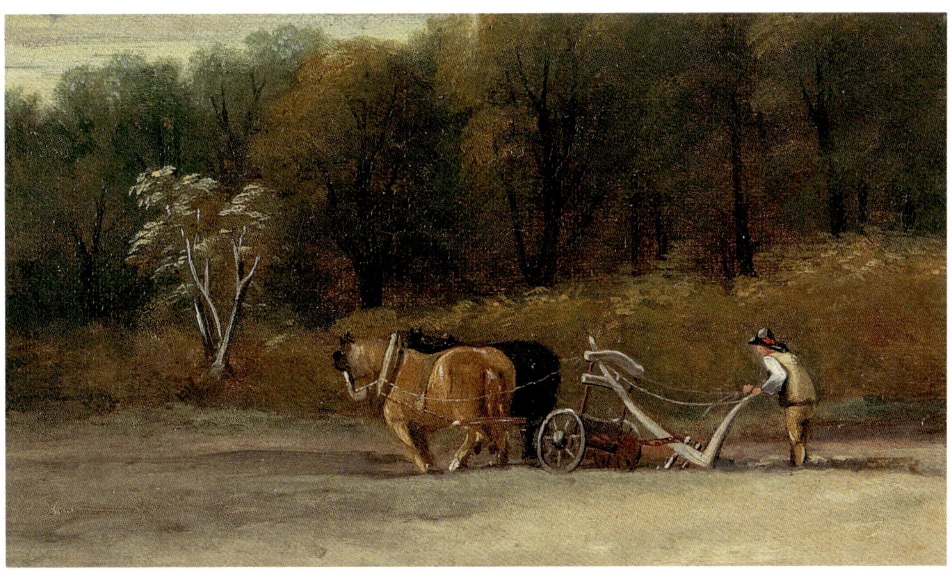

FIG. 10 John Constable, *Ploughing Scene in Suffolk*, 1824–25 (detail of plate 16)

was commissioned by Henry Greswolde Lewis to depict both the mansion and its owner's thirteen-year-old ward (perhaps Lewis's illegitimate daughter), Mary Freer (plate 3). Constable returned in 1820, when he created a more dramatic image of Malvern Hall in sharply receding perspective (plate 22). Adept at portraying cherished animals, as in *Golding Constable's Black Riding-Horse* (plate 4), Constable would not consider becoming an animalier like his contemporary James Ward. It must be landscape.

Although Constable sketched from nature, in early years he generally retreated to the studio to prepare landscapes for exhibition. This was the procedure used for *Ploughing Scene in Suffolk*, a composition that Constable painted twice: first in 1814–15 and again in 1824–25 (fig. 10), after the first version was altered by another hand. It focuses on the distant figure of a solitary ploughman, emphasizing the timeless cycle of rural labor. Working from detailed drawings on the first version, in his dark, cold London premises in the early months of 1814, Constable expressed grave dissatisfaction with his method, admitting that the painting lacked the lifelike qualities he sought, particularly the summer light. He proclaimed himself to be "determined to finish a small picture on the spot." That spring he confided to his mentor, the older painter Joseph Farington (1747–1821), that privately he had been "long occupied in painting Landscapes from nature." Now it was time to go public with this innovative method.

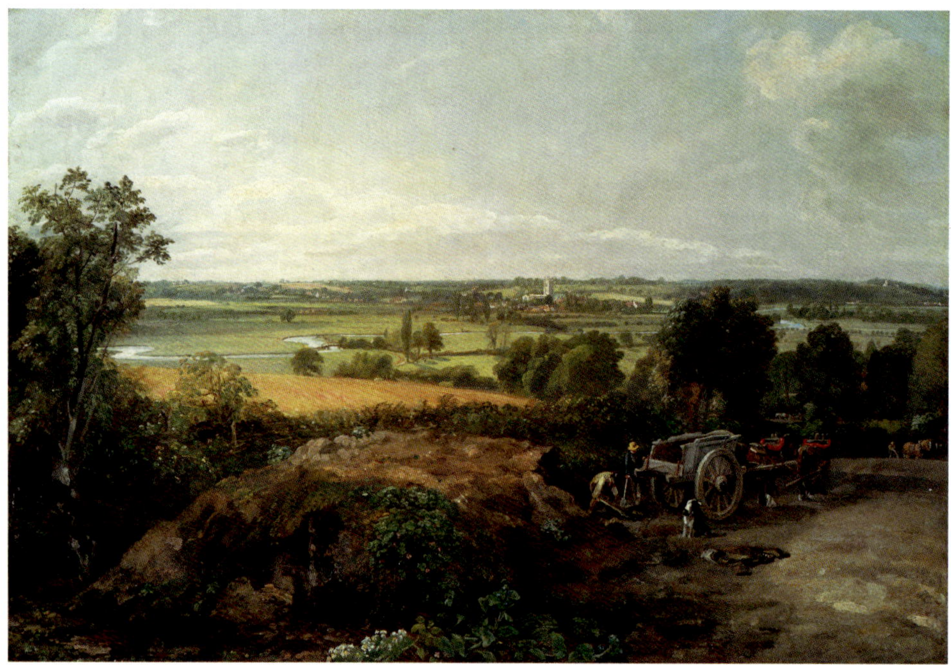

FIG. 11 John Constable, *Stour Valley and Dedham Church*, ca. 1815, oil on canvas, 21⅞ × 30⅝ in. (55.6 × 77.8 cm). Museum of Fine Arts, Boston

At the Royal Academy's exhibition of 1815, he displayed *Stour Valley and Dedham Church*, which he had painted painstakingly on the spot, using a portable easel (fig. 11). The small township of Dedham, Essex, its church tower just crossing the horizon, lies some way away in the center, beyond the water meadows and the snaking line of the River Stour. The painting's most striking feature, however, lies in the foreground: a large dunghill or "dungle" (as it was locally known), made of manure from cattle, which would be ploughed into the fields after harvest to fertilize the land. This fastidious insistence on the local and particular marked a brave, even insolent disavowal of academic orthodoxy as laid down in the foundational theory of the Royal Academy, Joshua Reynolds's *Discourses on Art*, in which earlier Dutch painters were castigated for representing the vulgar details of everyday life.

A year later Constable exhibited the sparkling *Wheat Field* (fig. 12), which represents the very same acreage seen in *Stour Valley and Dedham Church*. The view has now shifted to the right; it is later in the agricultural calendar. Fertilized by the nurturing manure ploughed into the stubble fields after the previous year's harvest, the crop has grown to ripeness. In the distance, male harvesters, visible

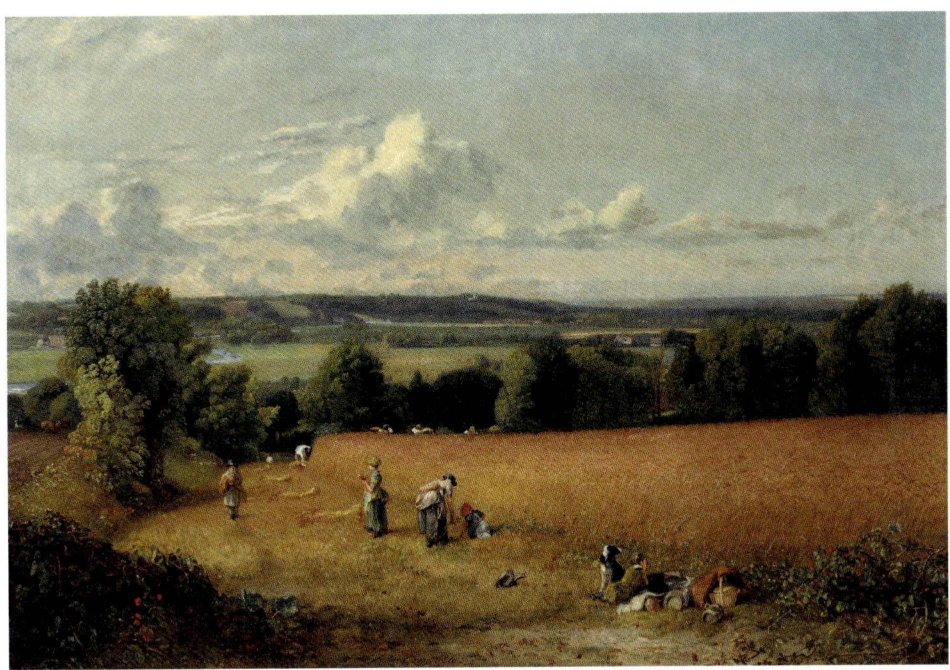

FIG. 12 John Constable, *The Wheat Field*, 1816, oil on canvas, 21½ × 30¾ in. (54.6 × 78.1 cm). The Clark Art Institute, Williamstown, Massachusetts

only from the waist up, are cutting the wheat with sickles; women and children are gleaning in the foreground. In terms of Constable's own cycle of labor, *The Wheat Field* brought to glorious ripeness the project of a "natural painture."

Like many rural Tories of the period, Constable decried the changes in rural life now known as the agricultural revolution. Most significant was enclosure, by which the medieval open-field system was replaced by modern patterns of ownership, consolidating the holdings of larger landowners and marginalizing the peasantry. By increasing food production, enclosure ensured that a growing population, based in cities, could be fed. Its cost, however, was a dissolution of traditional social relations, a development that Constable lamented. *The Wheat Field* offers a last glimpse of the old times, where an organic society supported by social rather than economic relationships was blessed (as Constable saw it) by natural bounty.

Constable's Tory rural idyll, if it ever really existed, dissolved before his very eyes. After the end of the Napoleonic Wars, in 1815, Britain faced a deep economic depression, repressive government, and demands for rapid social and political change. *The Wheat Field* was exhibited at the Royal Academy in 1816 and, the very next year, East Bergholt was enclosed. As times became harder for agricultural laborers, a period of violent agricultural unrest descended on the southern counties.

This was also a time of personal transformation for Constable. After a courtship of seven years and against the strong resistance of her family, in October 1816 he married Maria Bicknell (1788–1828) at St. Martin-in-the-Fields Church, in London. Thereafter, London would be the main focus of Constable's life, even as his imagination still yearned for Suffolk.

ACADEMIC AMBITIONS

Beginning in 1818, Constable embarked upon a series of large-scale works (the "six-footers"), mainly painted in his London studio. Compositions of enormous ambition and resonance, these were realized through the innovative use of preparatory works. From his earliest experiments in art-making, Constable made sketches outdoors; some were supple and confident studies in pencil, fewer in watercolor. His finest sketches, however, were swiftly painted in oil. These remarkable works, increasingly free and gestural as time went by, are distinctive to Constable. A further, startling innovation was Constable's practice of creating freely painted sketches on canvases as large as the exhibited paintings. These allowed him to maintain the vibrant energy of the smaller sketches but at exhibition scale. The flicker of the sun through passing clouds, captured in a small sketch, could now enliven paintings later prepared for exhibition with a meticulously detailed finish. So successful was *The White Horse* (1819, Frick Collection) at the exhibition of 1819 that Constable was elected an associate member of the Royal Academy—an indelible, if belated, imprimatur of professional success.

With mounting confidence, Constable submitted a second six-footer to the Academy in 1820 (fig. 13). Again, it depicted the River Stour, this time at Stratford St. Mary, a village near Dedham notable for its charming old watermill, which, in a development Constable would have doubtless deplored, was replaced by a modern brick building in 1825. Some elements of the composition appear in a vertical oil sketch made on site as early as 1811. Around 1819 he reworked the sketch in the studio, employing hasty, energetic brushstrokes, this time using a small, horizontal format (fig. 14). Constable made the leap to a six-foot canvas, on which he made a large sketch, not intended for public display, that once again was painted quickly with vibrant brushstrokes (plate 17). The viewer is positioned on the river bank by a sluice near the old waterwheel. After dwelling among

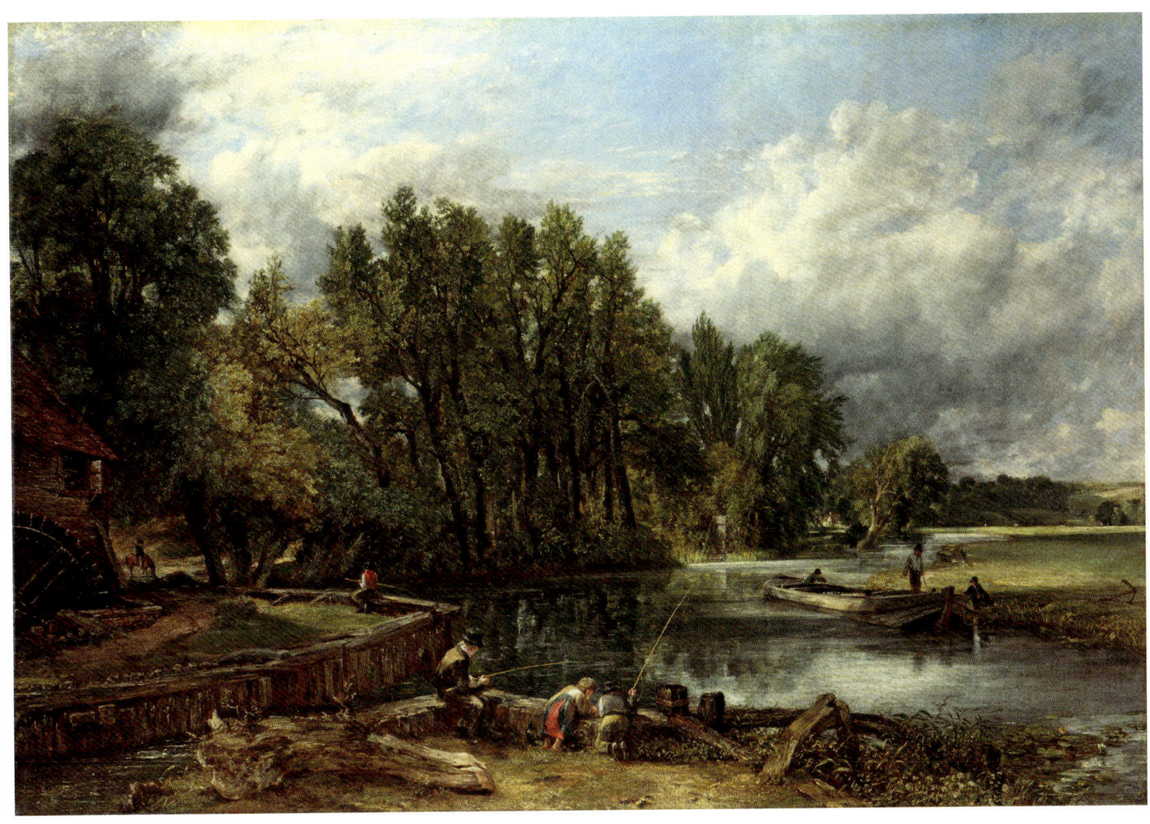

FIG. 13 John Constable, *Stratford Mill*, 1820, oil on canvas, 50 × 72 in. (127 × 182.9 cm). National Gallery, London

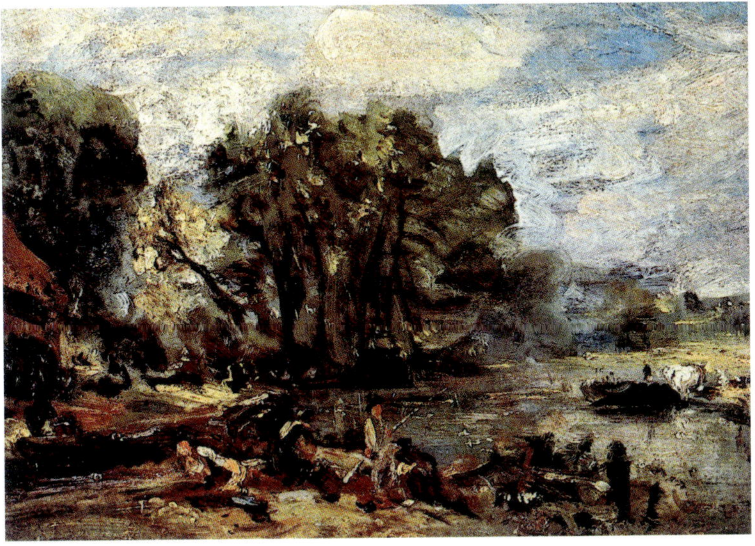

FIG. 14 John Constable, *Sketch for "Stratford Mill,"* ca. 1819, oil on canvas, 12 × 16½ in. (30.5 × 42 cm). Private collection

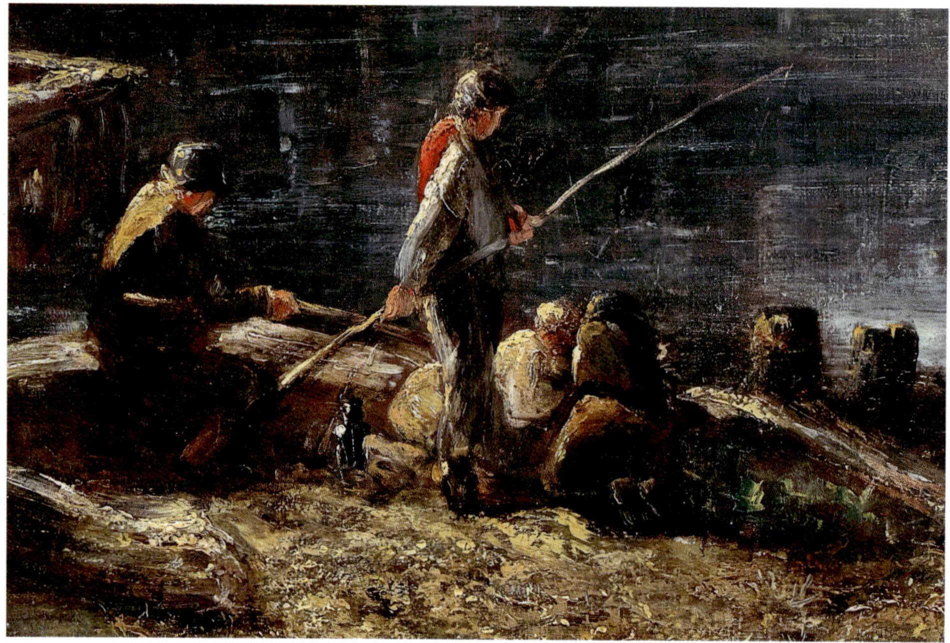

FIG. 15 John Constable, *Full-Size Sketch for "Stratford Mill,"* 1819–20 (detail of plate 17)

the fishermen in the foreground, the viewer's eye follows the curve of the Stour, which is brimming after recent rain. Shafts of sunlight penetrate the woods to the left, throwing a sparkling light on the river's surface. Unlike works made only a few years earlier, such as *The Wheat Field*, *Stratford Mill* is no longer a work of direct observation. Rooted in memory, it is a loving assemblage of recollections, arranged into a composition of symphonic complexity and amplitude.

In the full-size sketch, a boy in a red waistcoat is fishing in the foreground next to an older man, perhaps his grandfather (fig. 15). For the exhibited painting, Constable replaced him with two smaller children, as if to place this boy before the public would be too intimate a disclosure. In 1821 Constable wrote a heartfelt letter to his friend Reverend Fisher recalling his own attachment to this river, and perhaps we can find in that young fisherman a memory of Constable himself as a youth:

> *But I should paint my own places best—Painting is but another word for feeling. I associate my "careless boyhood" to all that lies on the banks of the Stour. They made me a painter (& I am gratefull) that is I had often thought of pictures of them before I had ever touched a pencil.*

With the majestic series of six-foot landscapes that occupied him during the 1820s, Constable had fused the personal and the local with the national, balancing freedom of expression with mastery of detail.

SKYING AND THE "GREAT LONDON"

From 1819 to 1826 Constable spent the dark winters in his London studio house with Maria and their growing family; but they usually summered in Hampstead. Only three miles north of the city, this outer suburb was attractive to the painter because of its extensive heath, a park with excellent views both toward and away from London. As he wrote to Fisher, he could "above all see nature—& unite a town & country life." Here Constable produced an astonishing corpus of oil sketches that focus on the play of light over the heath, some recording the terrain, others silhouetting trees against stormy skies (plates 34, 29). The heath was a place of husbandry but also leisure, much used for health-giving rambles (plate 30).

Constable memorably declared the sky to be the "chief *'Organ of sentiment'*" within a landscape, and now he concentrated on the sky alone, moving paint quickly to capture the scudding clouds before they disappeared. It was in Hampstead that Constable's interest in the sky took on a newly scientific, indeed ecological, dimension, as Nicholas Robbins explains later in this book. Even this interest was inflected by the rapid changes around him. These clouds were not a purely natural phenomenon: Many were darkened with carbon particles from the city's sooty fires and industrial chimneys.

Although he never became fully accustomed to London life, Constable addressed the modern metropolis in the largest of all his paintings, *The Opening of Waterloo Bridge ("Whitehall Stairs, June 18th, 1817")*, which, after fifteen years of uneasy labor, was finally exhibited in 1832 (fig. 16). The ostensible subject is one of metropolitan and imperial triumph—the opening of a grand new bridge designed by John Rennie, commemorating the victory of the Duke of Wellington and his allies over Napoleon at Waterloo. The prince regent led the patriotic jamboree, accompanied by soldiers in bright uniforms. The red and gold standard of the mayor of London's barge is positioned in Constable's composition directly beneath the dome of St. Paul's Cathedral. The painting celebrates the links between the monarchy, the military, the Anglican Church, and the financiers of the City of London. The artistic establishment, too, is prominent: The facade of Somerset House, home of the Royal Academy, is picked out by shafts of sunlight near the center of the canvas. The bridge itself, denoted by ruled lines and

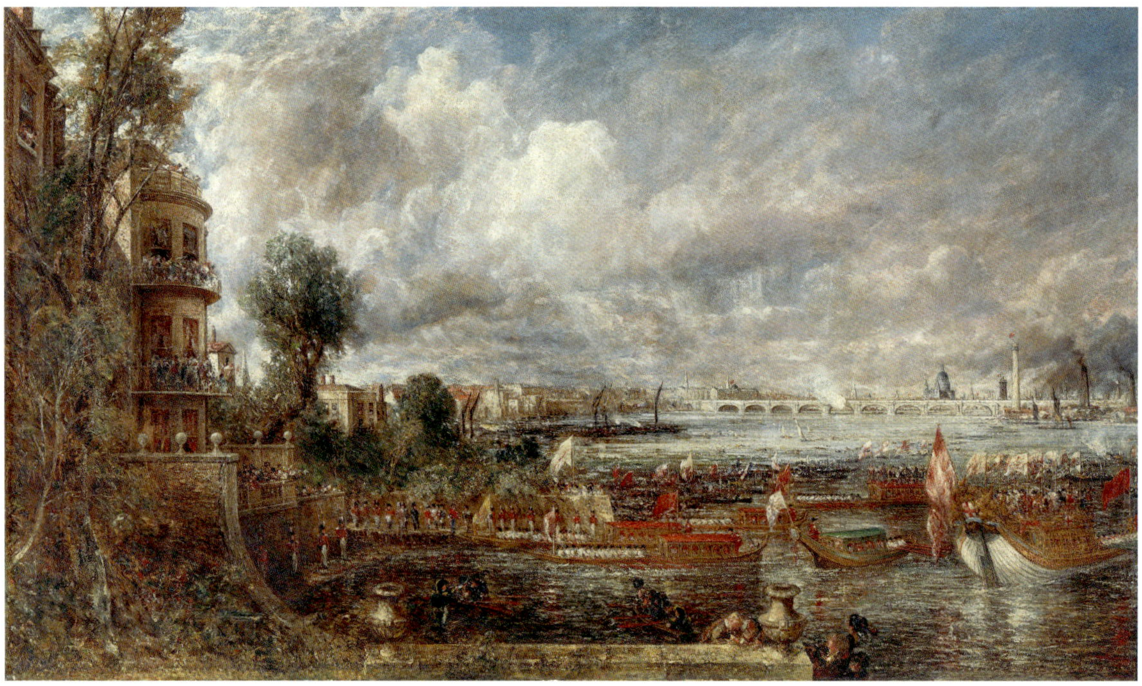

FIG. 16 John Constable, *The Opening of Waterloo Bridge ("Whitehall Stairs, June 18th, 1817")*, 1832, oil on canvas, 51½ × 85⅞ in. (130.8 × 218 cm). Tate Britain, London

depicted with brilliant white, is an unmistakable symbol of modernity. Standing on that very bridge, Constable made a bright sketch looking toward St. Paul's, for once caught up in the city's energy (plate 36).

Constable struggled for years to complete *The Opening of Waterloo Bridge*. In a highly finished version, now at Yale, half the size of the final painting, he had almost resolved his difficulties (plate 37), but the brilliance and glitter of the final version still eluded him. By February 1832 Constable could write, "I am dashing away at the great London," before sending the picture to the Royal Academy. The finished work reveals Constable's technique at its most extreme. Even his friend and biographer Charles Robert Leslie felt that Constable "had indulged in the vagaries of the palette knife . . . to excess" in pursuit of the "indispensable quality of the brightness of nature." Acknowledging its unusually vivid colors, Constable called it "my Harlequin's Jacket." *Waterloo Bridge* hung at the Royal Academy close to Turner's pale, atmospheric marine painting *Helvoetsluys* (fig. 17), leading to a celebrated altercation on varnishing day. It is recalled here by an eyewitness:

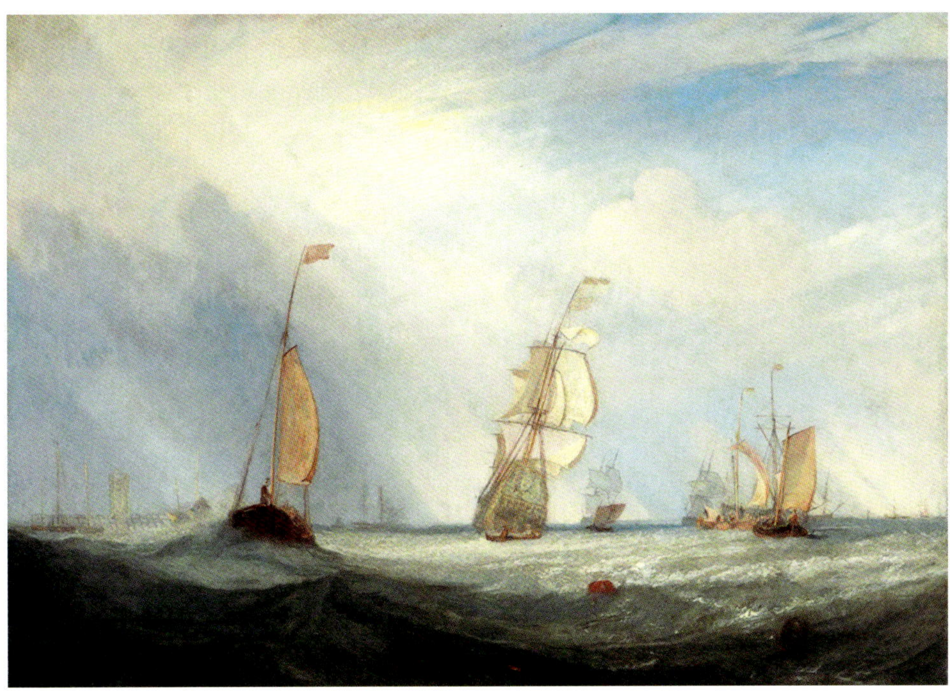

FIG. 17 J.M.W. Turner (English, 1775–1851), *Helvoetsluys;—the City of Utrecht, 64, Going to Sea*, 1832, oil on canvas, 36 × 48 in. (91.4 × 122 cm). Fuji Museum, Tokyo

> *A sea piece by Turner was next to it—a grey picture, beautiful and true, but with no positive colour in any part of it. Constable's picture seemed as if painted with liquid gold and silver, and Turner came several times into the room while he was heightening with vermilion and lake the decorations and flags of the city barges. Turner stood behind him, looking from the "Waterloo" to his own picture; and putting a round daub of red lead, somewhat bigger than a shilling, on his grey sea, went away without a word. The intensity of the red lead, made more vivid by the coolness of his picture, caused even the vermilion and lake of Constable to look weak. I came into the room just as Turner left it. "He has been here," said Constable, "and fired off a gun."*

Although *Waterloo Bridge* began as a work of national celebration, the final canvas is an ambivalent, even skeptical, response to contemporary England. Constable was hostile to the Whig-Liberal government under Charles Grey and, notably, to the Reform Act of 1832, which ushered in a limited form of democracy. The aging painter foresaw a dystopian future, with power handed to the "rabble and dregs of the people . . . and the slimy marshes of Chelsea and Paddington & St Pancras." Environmental disaster and social upheaval were linked in his mind. The most dramatic passage in the painting lies in right margin of the composition at the south end of the bridge: Here, shot towers belch black smoke, which mixes with the blustery clouds to form a menacing backdrop, echoed in the dark undertones of the polluted Thames water in the foreground. One of these towers was built after 1817, indicating that the painting's larger subject was modern London, perhaps modernity itself.

The last decades of his career would see a darkening of Constable's worldview: Heightened emotions shaped his work. He became increasingly preoccupied with the mounting tensions between traditional life and modern society, between rural and urban. Landscape painting was a tense business in an industrial age. Constable continued to revisit Hampstead as a subject even in his last years. A small masterpiece, *Sir Richard Steele's Cottage, Hampstead*, also exhibited in 1832, embodies these themes (plate 35). The picturesque house of the late seventeenth-century Irish writer stands in relief against the uniform gray mass of London's slate roofs. The roadway seems to transport the figures on a stagecoach from a comforting rural past to an uncertain metropolitan and industrial future; above, smoke again darkens the clouds.

THE CASTLE AND THE SOOT BAG

In 1814 Constable toured the south of Essex, the county adjacent to Suffolk that hugs the northern edge of the Thames estuary. He made a study in pencil of Hadleigh Castle, recording the two standing towers, the surrounding landscape, and a stormy sky with seagulls circling. Fifteen years later, he transformed the study into a large exhibition painting. First, he painted an oil sketch in the studio suggesting the overall composition and light effects (plate 39). Unlike the Hampstead sky studies, this is not an example of spontaneous observation but a swiftly executed work marshaling recollections of a scene into a viable composition. There followed a grand oil sketch, the same size as the final canvas but with a rough and extraordinarily turbulent paint surface, largely applied, quite violently, with the palette knife (fig. 18). In the magisterial exhibited version, the startling lighting effect of bright sunshine through fast-moving clouds was once again achieved by the obsessive use of white highlights (plate 38).

The ruined castle on its rough escarpment, buffeted by the wind, offered a profound metaphor for Constable's sense of loss, personal and national. His return to the subject may have been precipitated by the death of Maria, of tuberculosis, in November 1828 at the age of forty, leaving seven young children. "Hourly

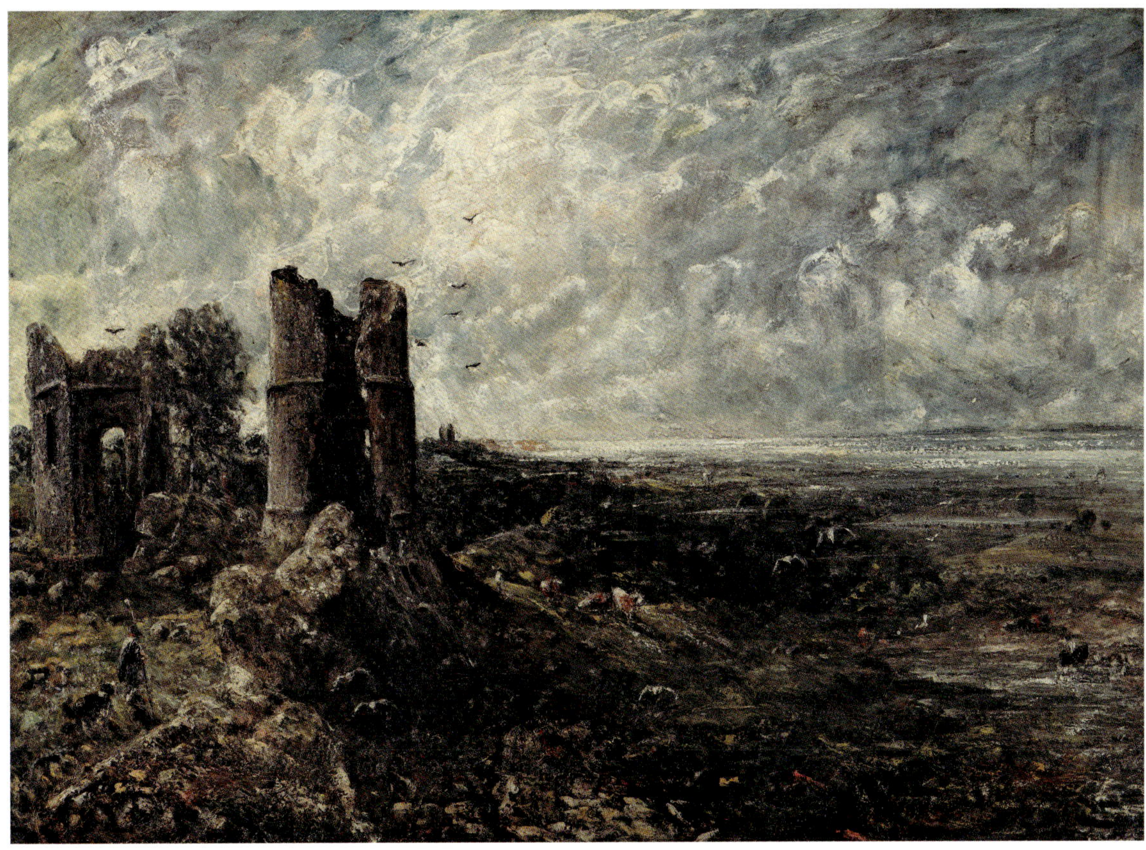

FIG. 18 John Constable, *Sketch for "Hadleigh Castle,"* ca. 1828–29, oil on canvas, 48¼ × 65⅞ in. (122.6 × 167.3. cm). Tate Britain, London

do I feel the loss of my departed Angel," he wrote the following month, as he began this painting. Election to full membership of the Royal Academy came too late to please him: "It has been delayed until I am solitary, and cannot impart it," he wrote. The gloom was political as well as personal. Constable in 1829 was unimpressed by the global reach of British power and wealth—hinted at by the merchant ships seen in glittering sunlight on the distant Thames. By abandoning its traditional social hierarchies, the nation, he felt, courted catastrophe. At Hadleigh, the castle, immemorial symbol of royal and aristocratic dominion, of noblesse oblige, stands neglected. The countryside—so lovingly cultivated and managed in his earlier work—is run to ruin, a state shared, it seemed to Constable, by both the nation and the artist himself.

Constable thought highly enough of *Hadleigh Castle* to include it in *English Landscape*. The plate, published in July 1832, captures the stormy chiaroscuro of

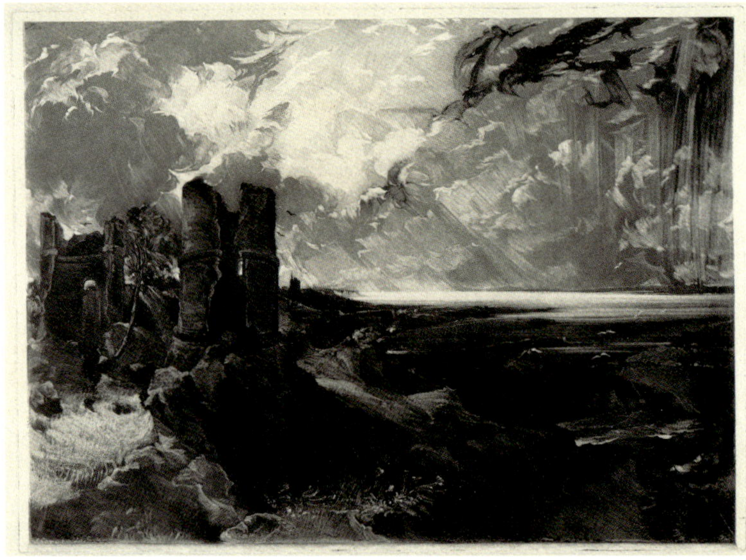

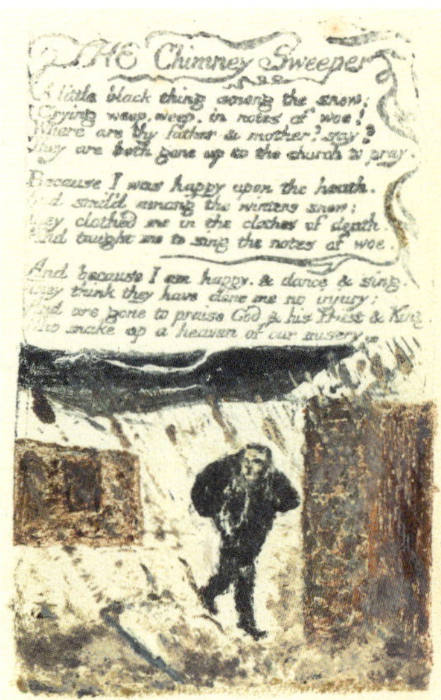

FIG. 19 David Lucas after John Constable, *Hadleigh Castle, Large Plate*, 1830–32, mezzotint: progress proof, 15¼ × 19½ in. (38.7 × 49.5 cm). Yale Center for British Art, Paul Mellon Collection

FIG. 20 William Blake (English, 1757–1827), *The Chimney Sweeper* (from *Songs of Innocence and of Experience*), 1794, color-printed relief etching, with hand coloring in watercolor, 7¼ × 4¾ in. (18.4 × 12.1 cm). Yale Center for British Art, Paul Mellon Collection

the exhibited painting. Lucas so admired the composition that he had already begun, at his own expense, a larger, even more dramatic, mezzotint (plate 66) based on the freer, full-size oil sketch. Of an early proof of this larger plate, Constable wrote in February 1830, "It is mighty fine—though it looks as if all the chimney sweepers in Christendom had been at work on it, & thrown their soot bags up in the air" (fig. 19). No one illuminated the harshness of urban modernity more clearly than the London chimney sweep, the miserable urchin seen in William Blake's *Songs of Innocence and of Experience* (fig. 20). Constable's invocation of factory-age carbon pollution in relation to his picture of a medieval castle reminds us once again of the tense, unresolved binaries of country and city, agriculture and industry, tradition and modernity that underlie his work.

THE CATHEDRAL AND THE RAINBOW

Although the "great London," begun years earlier, was first exhibited in 1832, *Salisbury Cathedral from the Meadows*, shown the previous year, stands as the last of

Constable's six-footers (fig. 21). A magisterial, valedictory statement, it offered the "fullest impression of the compass of his art," Constable avowed. The painter had been a regular visitor to Salisbury since 1811, where he was the guest of the bishop, Dr. John Fisher (1748–1825). First introduced to this grand prelate as a young man in Suffolk in 1798, Constable benefited from his patronage; the bishop's nephew, another churchman, also called John Fisher, became perhaps Constable's closest friend and correspondent, and it was he who provided the telling Latin translation for *English Landscape*. The long history of England seemed close at hand in Salisbury. The cathedral was a magnificent Gothic structure known for its tall, slender spire. The painter revered the "venerable grandeur" of "religious edifices," none more than Salisbury Cathedral, admiring "the charm that the mellowing hand of time hath cast over them," which "gives them an aspect of extreme solemnity and pathos."

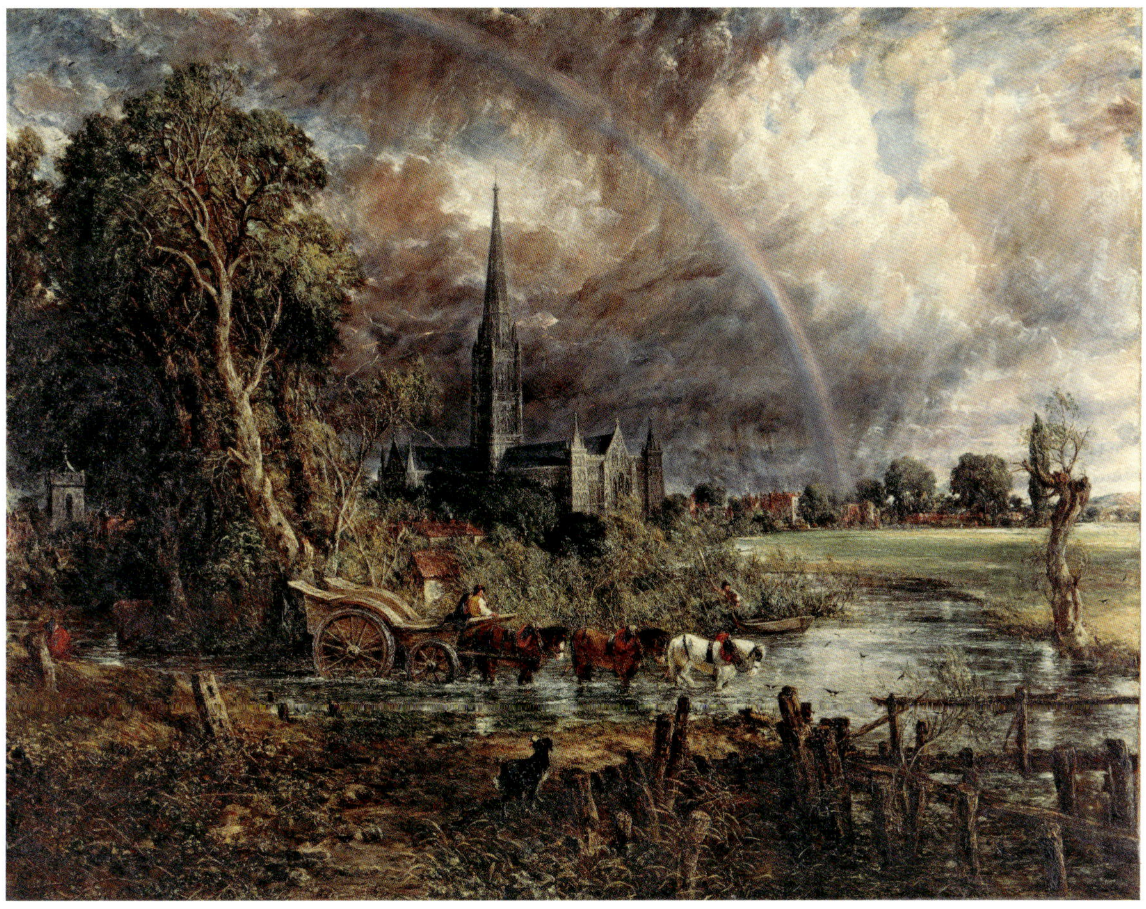

FIG. 21 John Constable, *Salisbury Cathedral from the Meadows*, exhibited 1831, oil on canvas, 60½ × 75⅜ in. (153.7 × 192 cm). Tate Britain, London

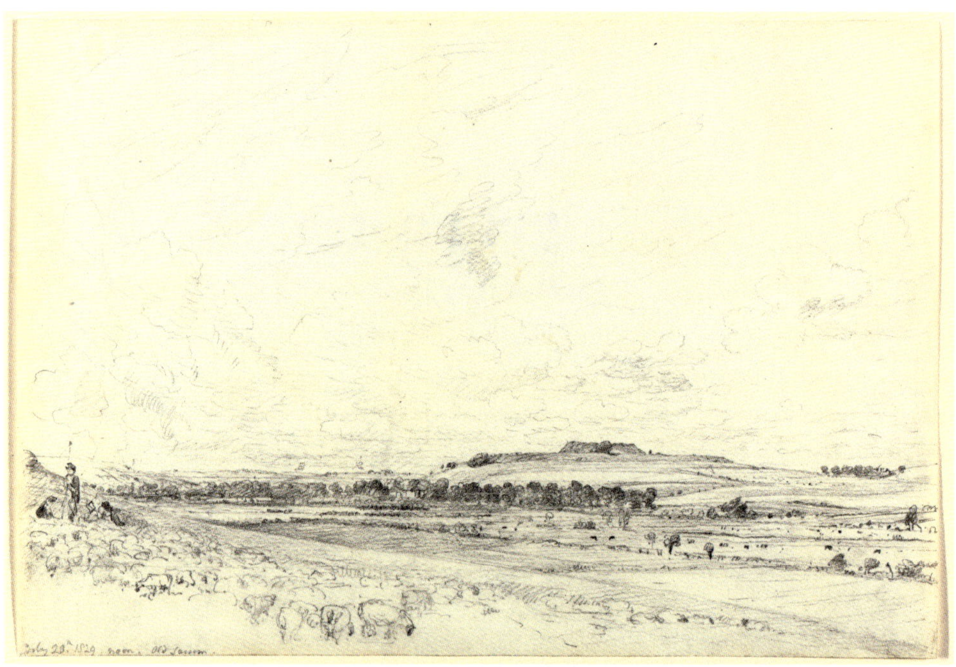

FIG. 22 John Constable, *Old Sarum at Noon*, 1829, graphite, 9⅛ × 13¼ in. (23.2 × 33.7 cm), Yale Center for British Art, Paul Mellon Collection

Salisbury lies close to sites with even deeper historical associations: Stonehenge, the subject of one of Constable's most dramatic exhibition watercolors (1829, Victoria and Albert Museum), and the Iron Age hill fort at Old Sarum. For *English Landscape*, Constable commissioned from Lucas a mezzotint after a stormy oil sketch of the fort (plate 61). This seems to have been based in turn on a precise, coolly analytical drawing, *Old Sarum at Noon*, made on July 20, 1829 (fig. 22). Constable's accompanying letterpress for *English Landscape* notes that Sarum once witnessed the "establishment of the feudal system" and lent its name to the traditional rites of the English church. Long abandoned, it had gained infamy as a so-called rotten borough, with local landholders sending two representatives to the House of Commons despite there being few, if any, voters resident in the constituency. The 1832 Reform Act swept away such picturesque anomalies, redistributing seats in parliament to the new manufacturing districts.

Salisbury Cathedral from the Meadows began with picturesque materials, the cathedral and its pleasing historic environs, which Constable recorded in a hasty pencil drawing (plate 54). The exhibited painting presents the scene in a radically different mode, that of the sublime. Constable generally eschewed this aesthetic category, which was rooted in the idea that fear and awe are the most powerful emotions. But the times demanded it. Constable was profoundly committed to the Anglican Church, which—like the medieval spire of Salisbury amid the lightning—he felt to be in mortal danger, both from the renewed influence of Roman Catholicism following the passing of the Catholic Emancipation Act of 1829 and from the insurgent Evangelical movement. The conflict of forces in society seems to find voice in the interaction of darkness and light, storm and sunshine. The timeless Georgic activities of the farmhand in the foreground have been interrupted (as in *The Hay Wain*) by a sudden flood: His cart is stalled and his team of six sturdy horses falters, unable to proceed.

After completing the full-size sketch for the painting, Constable added a rainbow. This optical phenomenon fascinated him: A vivid watercolor of 1827 presents a rainbow in stark relief against a gray-blue sky (plate 57). Its presence also declared a significant artistic affiliation, paying homage to *Landscape with Rainbow* (ca. 1636, Wallace Collection) by his beloved Rubens, which had been in London since 1802. Sunshine penetrates through the dark clouds, and despite Constable's pessimism about the modern world, the rainbow in *Salisbury Cathedral from the Meadows* surely signifies, in adversity, the possibility of redemption.

CONSTABLE AFTER MODERNISM

Constable's works now hold a secure place in the pantheon of art history. This was not always the case. Queen Victoria ascended to the throne in the year of Constable's death, 1837; led by the critic John Ruskin, Victorian taste preferred the work of his great rival, Turner. Advocacy came from an unlikely source: the bohemian artists of Paris. *The Hay Wain* was shown to acclaim at the Paris Salon in 1824, where the young Eugène Delacroix found its brilliant color and flickering light revelatory. Constable's influence can be seen in the French plein air painters of the Barbizon School of the mid-nineteenth century, such as Charles-François Daubigny (fig. 23). The Suffolk painter's dynamic brushwork and commitment to painting out of doors also lay in the ancestry of Impressionism. Toward the end of the nineteenth century, the rising status of Impressionist painting leveraged a major rehabilitation of Constable's reputation in Britain, according his work a celebrity it never held in his lifetime—an ironic twist of fate, perhaps, for the most English of painters.

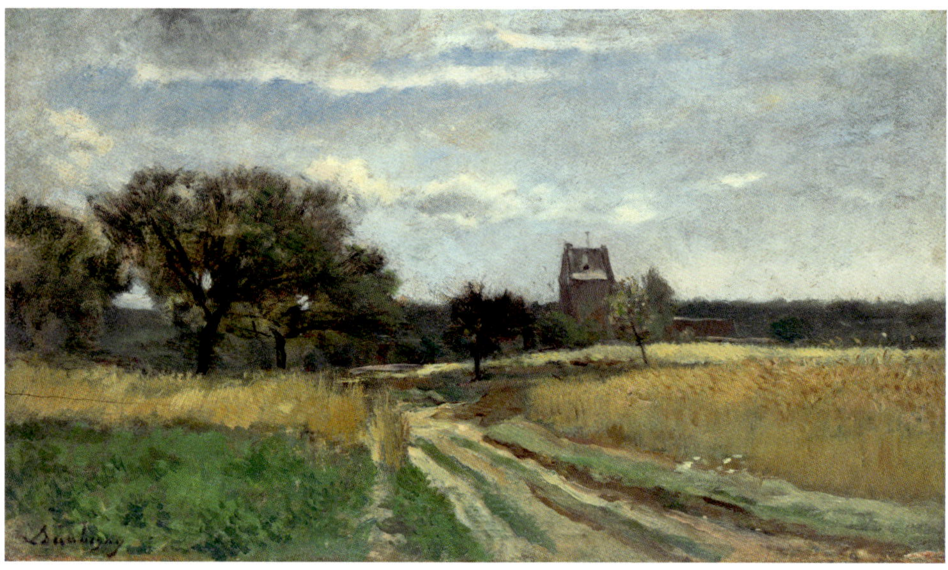

FIG. 23 Charles-François Daubigny (French, 1817–1878), *Landscape along a Country Road*, ca. 1860, oil on canvas, 8 × 13⅜ in. (20.2 × 33.8 cm). Yale University Art Gallery

This came at a cost. Modernist taste in the twentieth century admired Constable's gestural, expressionistic sketches but disavowed the finely wrought pictures exhibited in his lifetime. The curator of the Museum of Modern Art's 1956 exhibition *Masters of British Painting* pronounced, "[Constable] tried to appease the Royal Academy and its authorities by 'finishing' his canvases for exhibition—slicking over what appeared to the conventional eye to be the rough surface of his brushwork and the crude directness of his coloring." This account, persuasive in its day, has no purchase now that modernism itself seems merely another exhausted historical paradigm. The urgent modernity of Constable's art lies in his anxiety about nature, climate, and the environment in the face of industrial development, his sophisticated engagement with artistic tradition, and his willingness to embrace an openly emotive artistic practice. To take Constable seriously today is to give equal weight to work in every style and medium, the Academy set piece as much as the oil sketch, ink drawing, or mezzotint.

The philanthropist Paul Mellon (1907–1999), gathering works in the Cold War decades before presenting them to the YCBA in 1977, focused on acquiring a superb group of oil sketches, sky studies prominent among them (fig. 24). Although his taste was shaped by modernism, he added representative examples

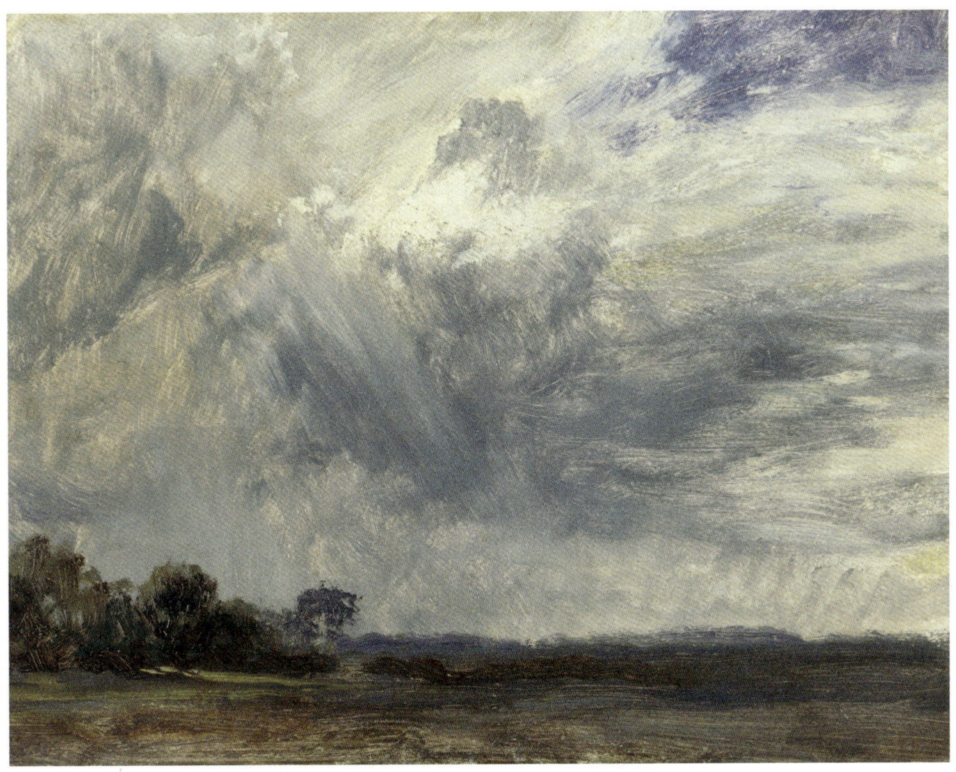

FIG. 24 John Constable, *Study of a Cloudy Sky*, ca. 1825, oil on paper mounted on millboard, 10⅜ × 13 in. (26.4 × 33 cm). Yale Center for British Art, Paul Mellon Collection

from across the artist's career in all mediums. Visitors to the YCBA, and readers of this book, can thus enjoy the full amplitude of Constable's creativity.

Constable asked David Lucas to do the impossible in the *English Landscape* mezzotints: to translate onto paper the astonishing range of mark-making, atmosphere, and mood encompassed in his landscape paintings; to reveal their euphoria and despair to a wide public. The selection of plates that follows aspires to do the same.

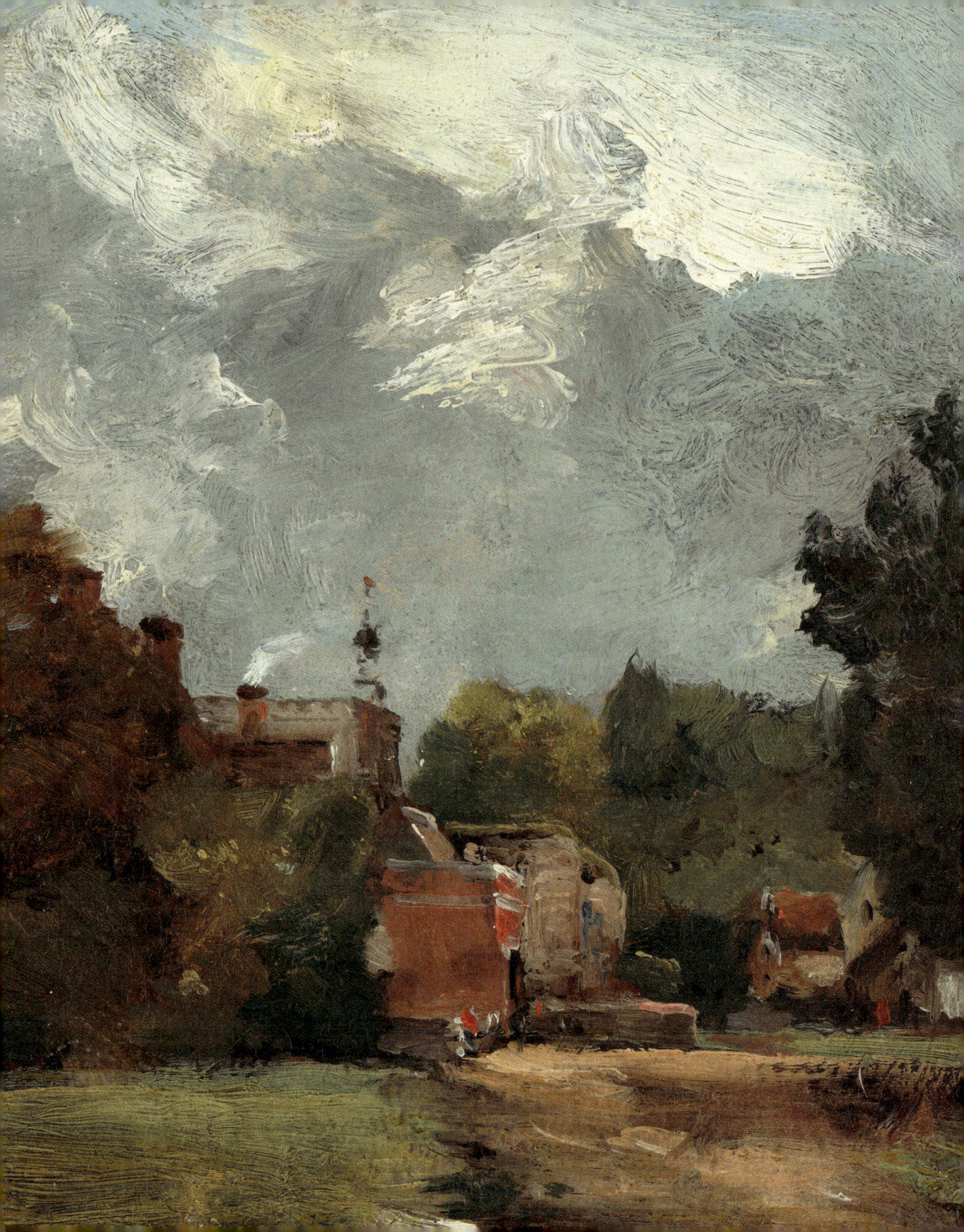

Early Paintings and Oil Sketches

From the beginning, Constable insisted on the value of "laborious studies," painted directly from nature. But what would a "natural painture" look like, and how would it be achieved? The first works he created on his return to East Bergholt in summer 1802 were not quick sketches. The result of intense observation, they were slowly painted, on the spot, using canvases of modest, portable scale. *Dedham Vale* is painted relatively thinly, with an occasional brushstroke of rich impasto drawing the eye to details such as the seated laborer at left, or the corner of a white building in the middle ground (plate 1).

The works that made possible Constable's transformation from a painstaking observer of local scenery to a visionary and transformative artist were small sketches in oil. English landscape painters, like gentleman amateurs, typically sketched in pencil or watercolor, often using a pocket-size sketchbook. But Constable discovered in the first decade of the century that he was most effective manipulating oil paint at speed on small wood panels, fragments of canvas, or, sometimes, on two sheets of thick paper, glued together and primed to receive the thick paint. In a panoramic study, dated to around 1809, of the house in which he was born, he revels in the contrast between the smooth meadow in the foreground, the massive trees, and, in a dramatic outburst of impasto, the clouds above (plate 6). Pencil might have revealed more architectural detail; watercolor perhaps could have articulated the boughs of the tree with greater fidelity. But the oil sketch captures both the mood of the place and the intensity of Constable's feelings for it. These small landscapes of association were charged with emotion. Constable wrote to Maria during their courtship: "You know I have succeeded most with my native scenes. They have always charmed me and I hope they always will—I wish not to forget early impressions."

East Bergholt Church 1809 (detail of plate 8)

With increasingly confident strokes of the brush, Constable affectionately captured familiar scenes—a barge on the river below Flatford Lock, like those owned by his father, Golding (plate 11); or a corner of East Bergholt Church where the family worshipped, seen from near their home (plate 8). Often a solitary figure stands in for the viewer: the shepherd shielding his eyes from the last rays of the setting sun (plate 12), or the wayfarer resting against a fallen tree on Fen Lane, East Bergholt (plate 9). The ancient bridleway slopes down to the River Stour, shaded by great trees, their foliage suggested by thickly impasted strokes of rich color.

There was nothing new in painting from the motif with oils: This technique was common among the international community of painters who gathered in Rome in the late eighteenth century around the charismatic French painter Claude-Joseph Vernet (1714–1789). Although he never went to Italy, Constable belongs within this artistic genealogy. British artists in Rome included Richard Wilson and Alexander Cozens (1717–1786), both of whom Constable admired. Wilson's student William Hodges (1744–1797) created remarkable oil sketches in the South Pacific while on Captain Cook's second voyage, and Wilson taught Joseph Farington, who became a mentor to Constable, as did George Beaumont, who studied with Cozens. Despite technical similarities, however, Constable harnessed the affective qualities of the medium in a distinctive, idiosyncratic fashion.

His early exhibited paintings, pieced together in the studio from sketches, were not always successful. A crisis was reached in winter 1813–14, when Constable was painting *Ploughing Scene in Suffolk*. Although the painting is filled with felicitous details, Constable found it "bleak," reflecting the winter light in his London studio, not that of the summer in Suffolk. The work illustrated here (plate 16) is a replica of that painting, made by Constable from 1824 to 1825, after the original, at the behest of its owner, had been partly repainted by another artist and damaged. The composition appears again in *English Landscape* with the title *A Summerland*—which identifies the subject as a field ploughed in summer to remain fallow until later planting (plate 60).

The plates that follow illustrate works from the Yale Center for British Art, Paul Mellon Collection, unless otherwise indicated.

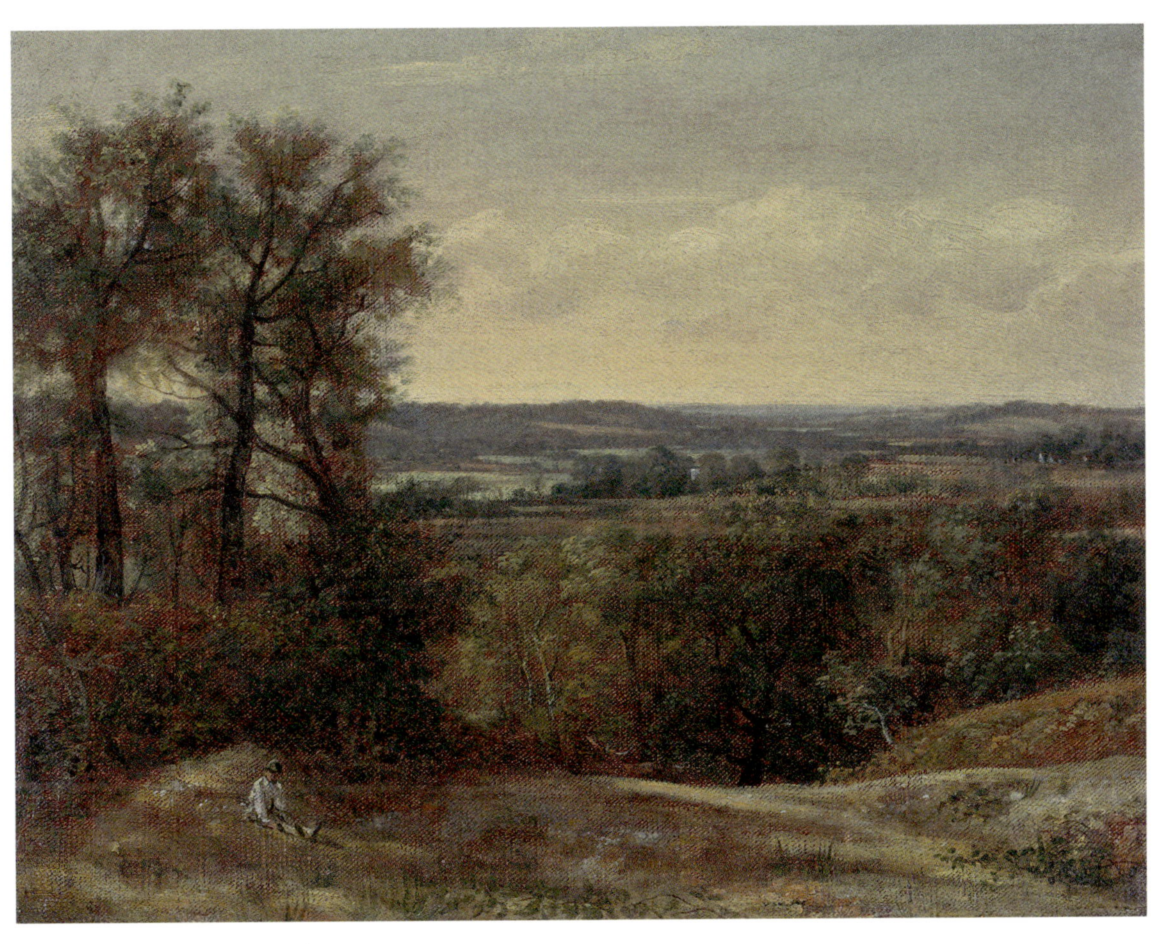

1

1
Dedham Vale 1802
oil on canvas, 13⅛ × 16⅜ in. (33.3 × 41.6 cm)

2

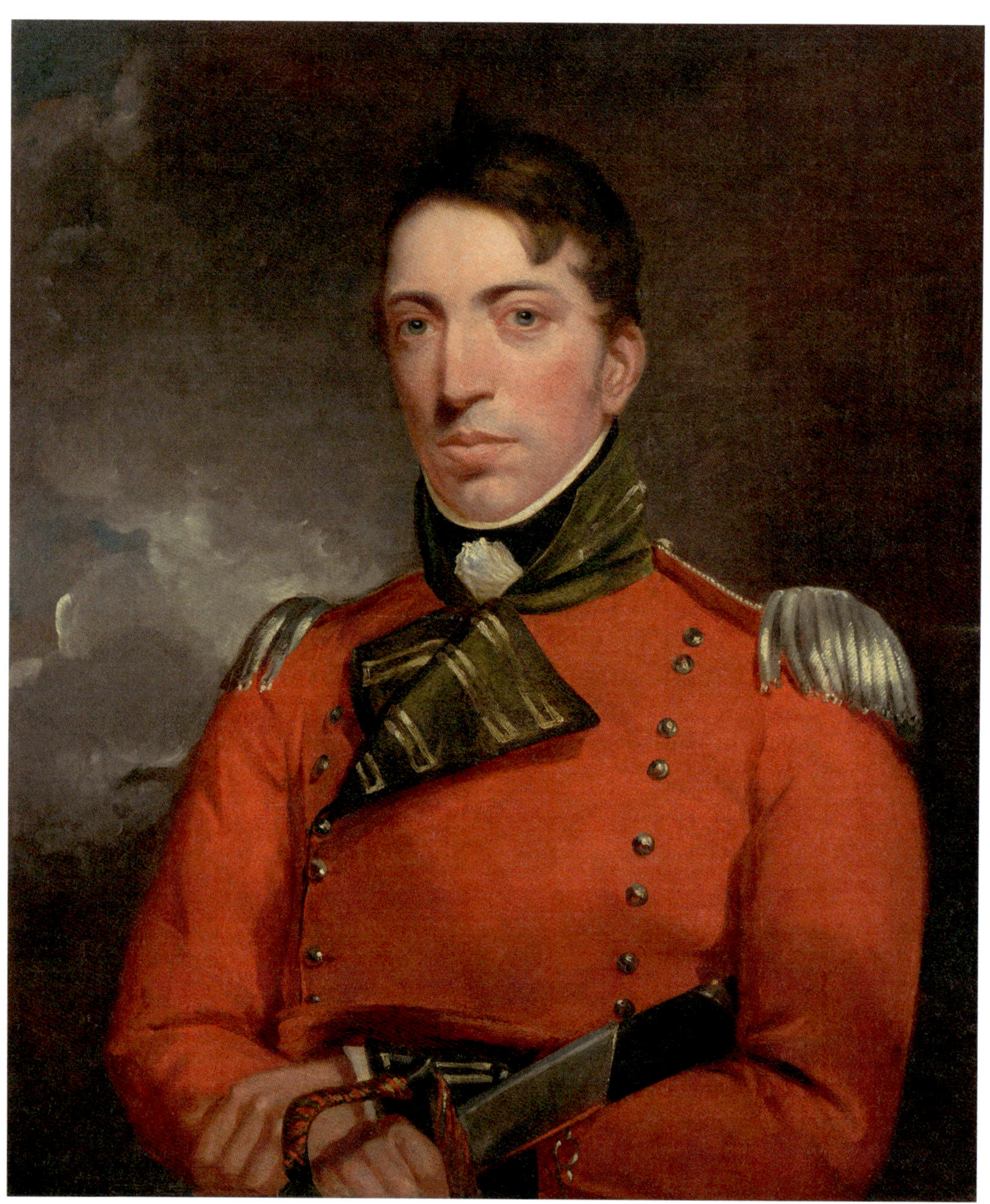

2
Captain Richard Gubbins 1804–5
oil on canvas, 30 × 25⅛ in. (76.2 × 63.8 cm)

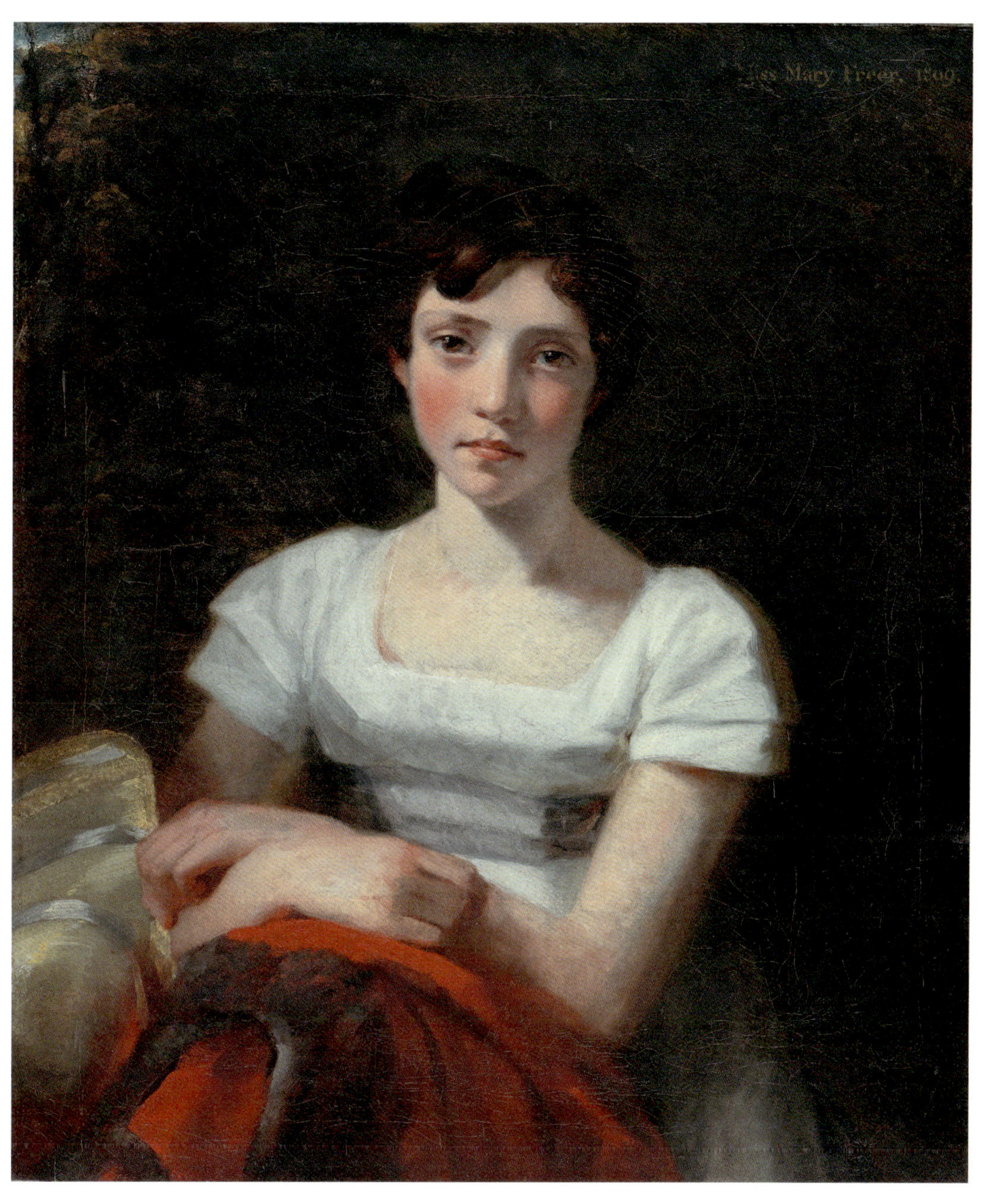

3

3
Mary Freer 1809
oil on canvas, 30 × 25 in. (76.2 × 63.5 cm)

4 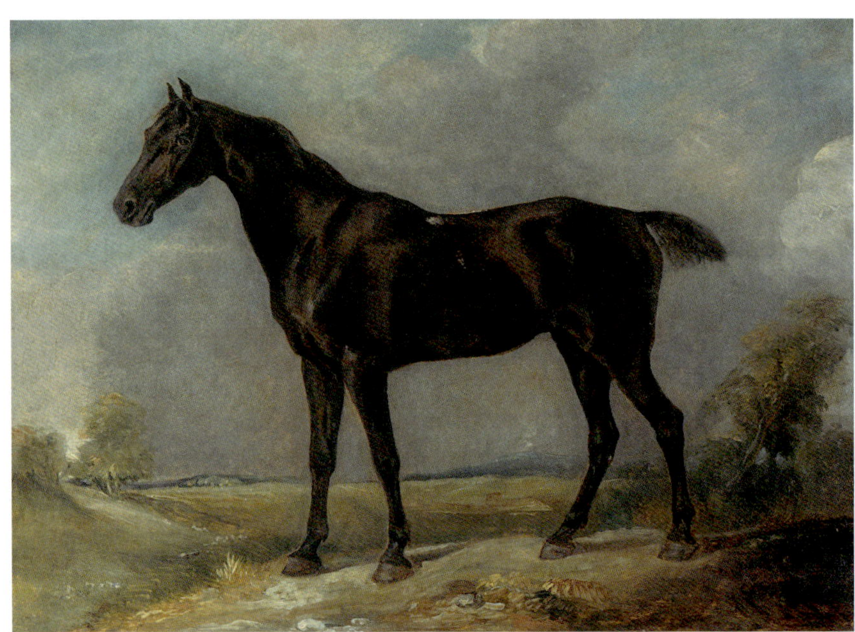

5 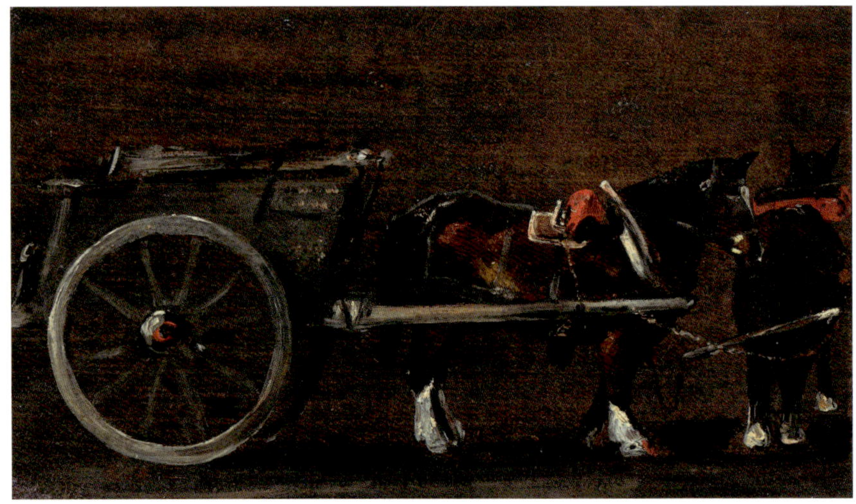

4
Golding Constable's Black Riding-Horse 1805–10
oil on panel, 14 × 18¼ in. (35.6 × 46.4 cm)

5
Horse and Cart ca. 1814
oil on canvas, mounted on board, 6⅜ × 10½ in. (16.2 × 26.7 cm)

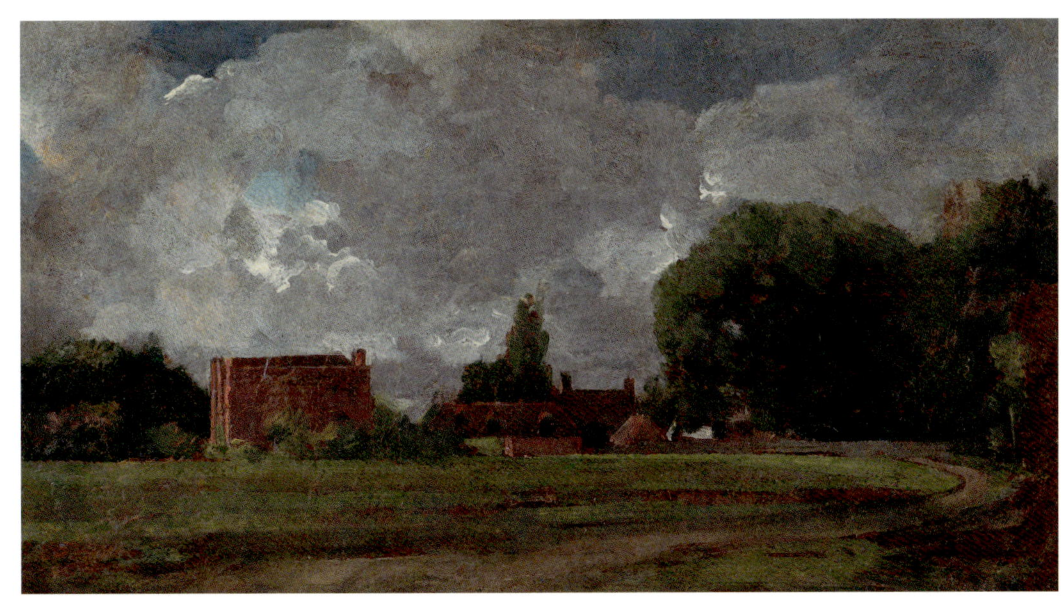
6

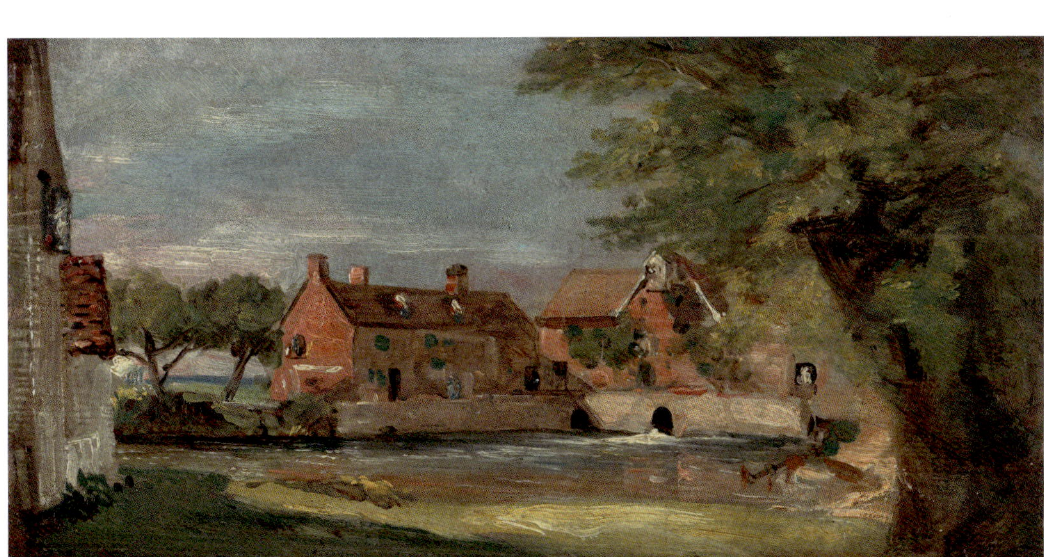
7

6
Golding Constable's House, East Bergholt: The Artist's Birthplace ca. 1809
oil on canvas, 5¾ × 10 in. (14.6 × 25.4 cm)

7
Flatford Mill 1810–11
oil on panel, 6½ × 11¾ in. (16.5 × 29.8 cm)

8

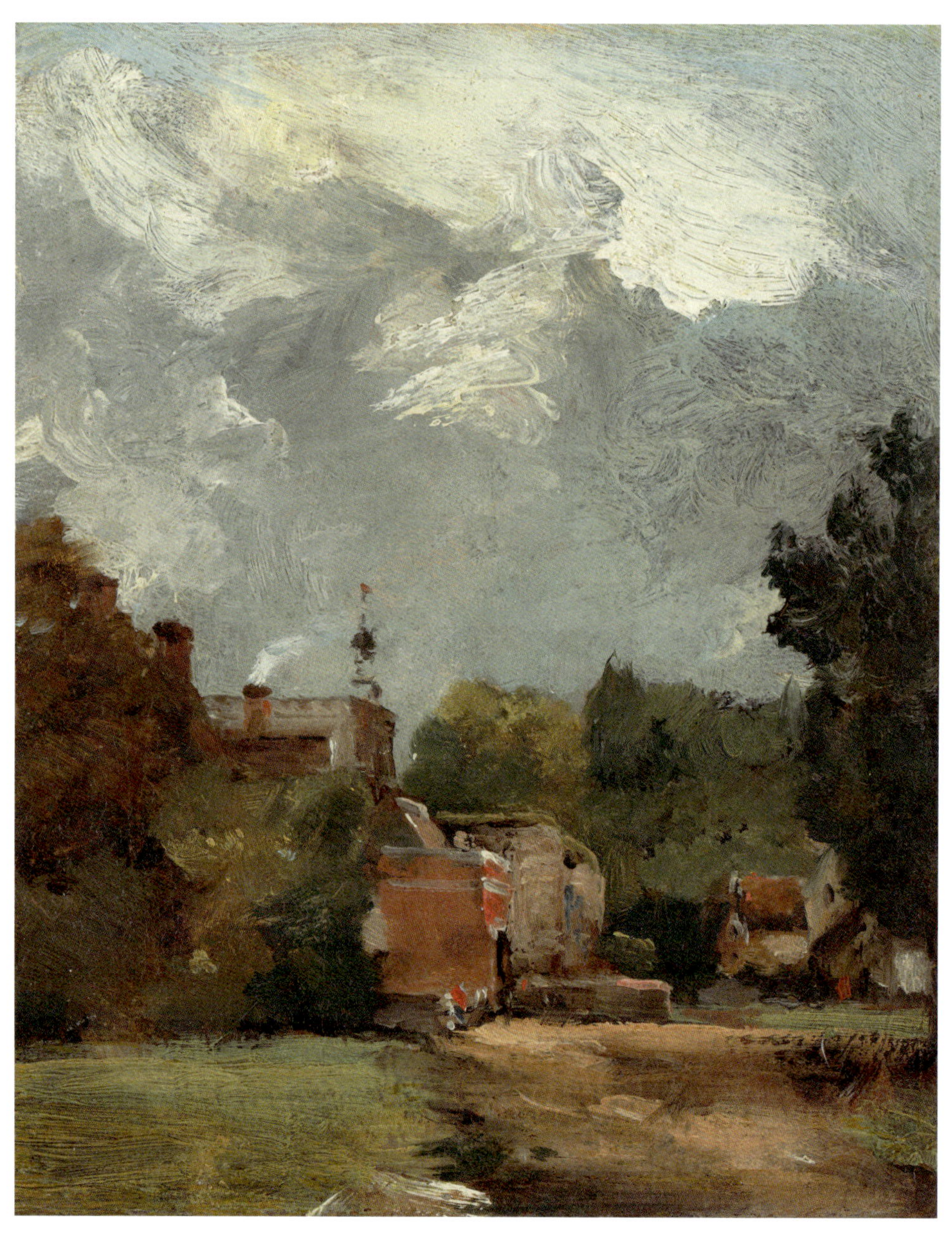

8

East Bergholt Church 1809

oil on paper, mounted on panel, 8 × 6¼ in. (20.2 × 15.7 cm)

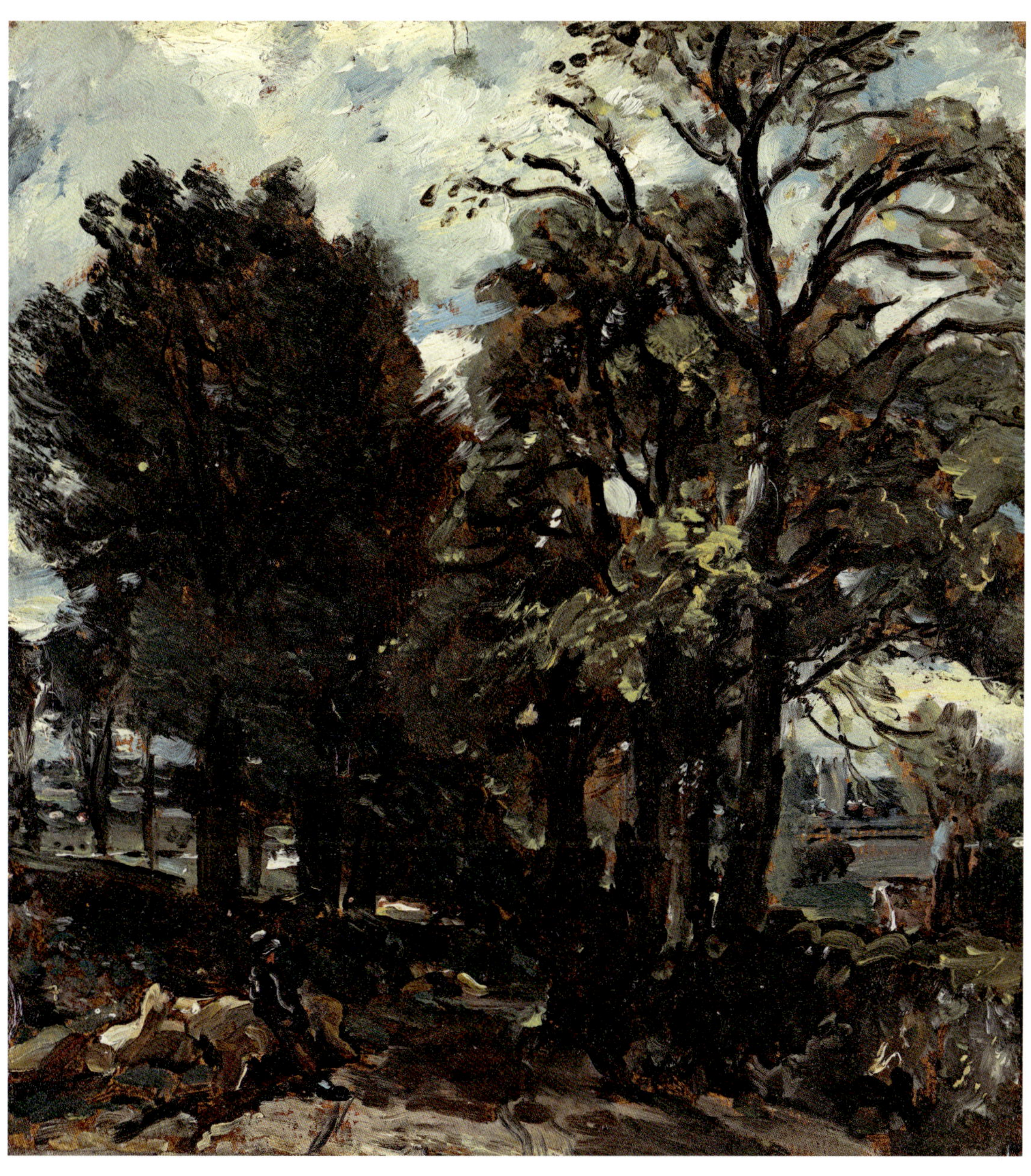

9

9
Fen Lane, East Bergholt ca. 1811
oil on paper, mounted on canvas, 8¾ × 7¾ in. (22.1 × 19.5 cm)

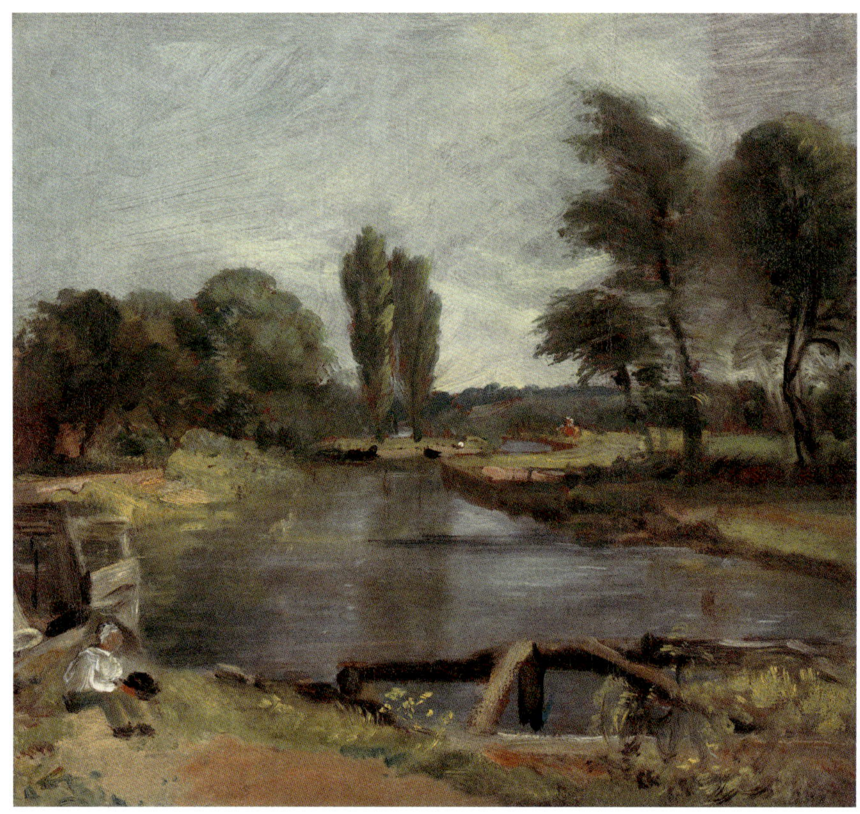
10

10
Flatford Lock 1810–11
oil on paper, mounted on canvas,
14½ × 14½ in. (36.8 × 36.8 cm)

11
Barge below Flatford Lock
ca. 1810
oil on canvas, 7¾ × 12¼ in.
(19.5 × 31.1 cm)

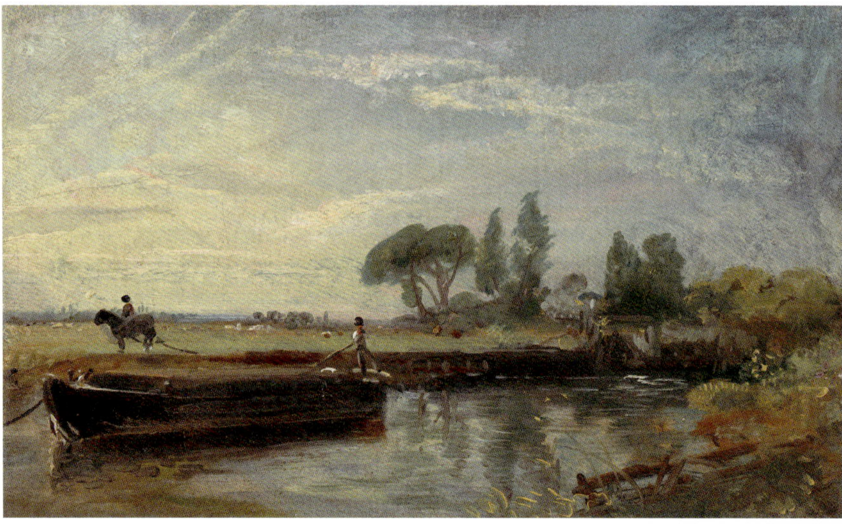
11

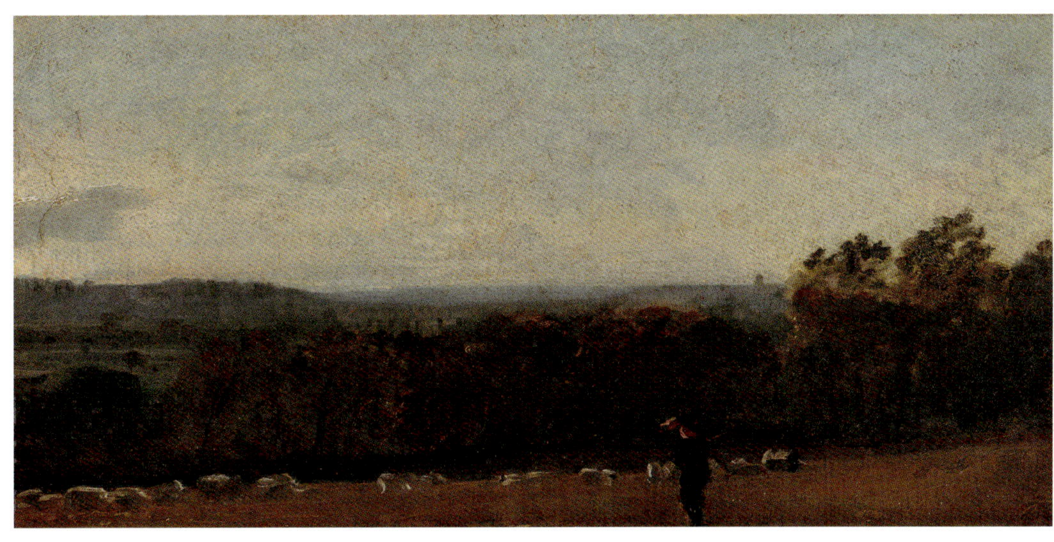

12

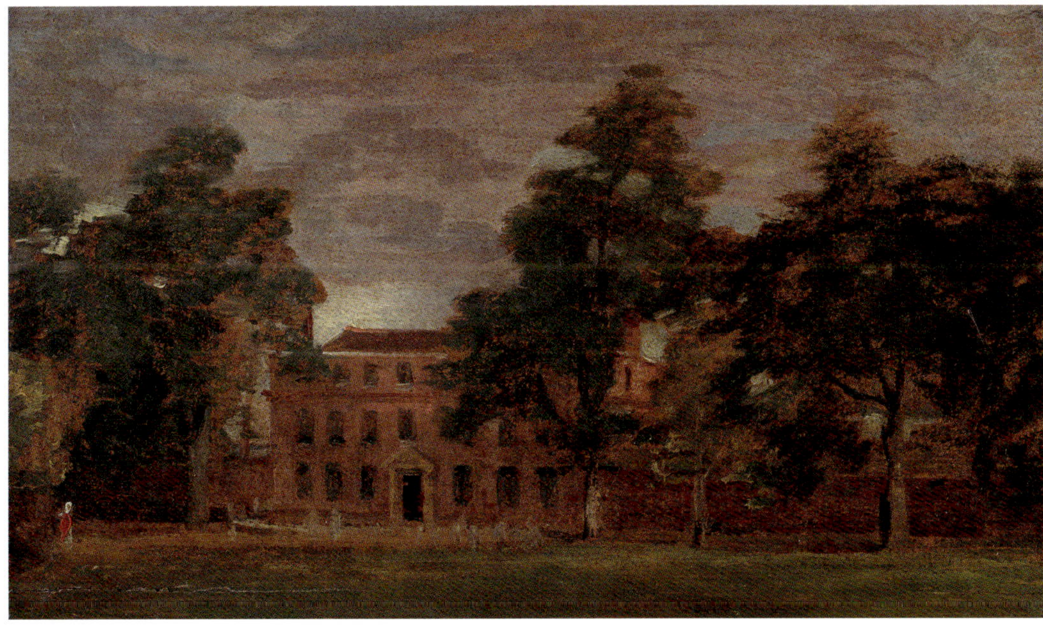

13

12
A Shepherd in a Landscape Looking across Dedham Vale towards Langham ca. 1811
oil on paper, mounted on canvas, 5⅞ × 11½ in. (14.9 × 29.2 cm)

13
West Lodge, East Bergholt 1813–16
oil on paper, mounted on panel, 5¾ × 11¾ in. (14.6 × 29.8 cm)

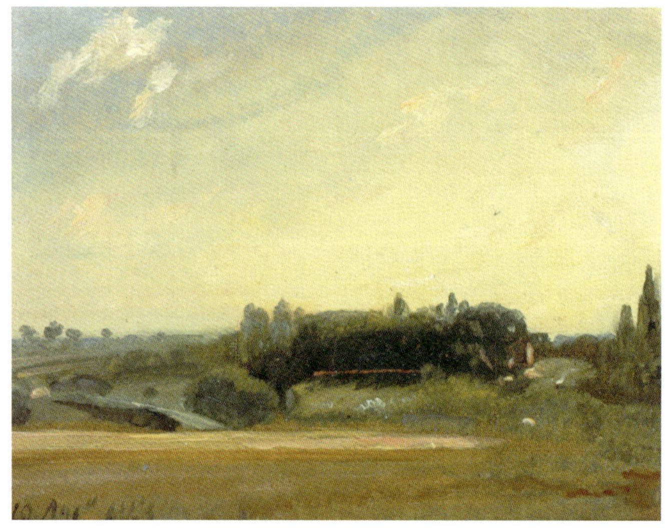

14

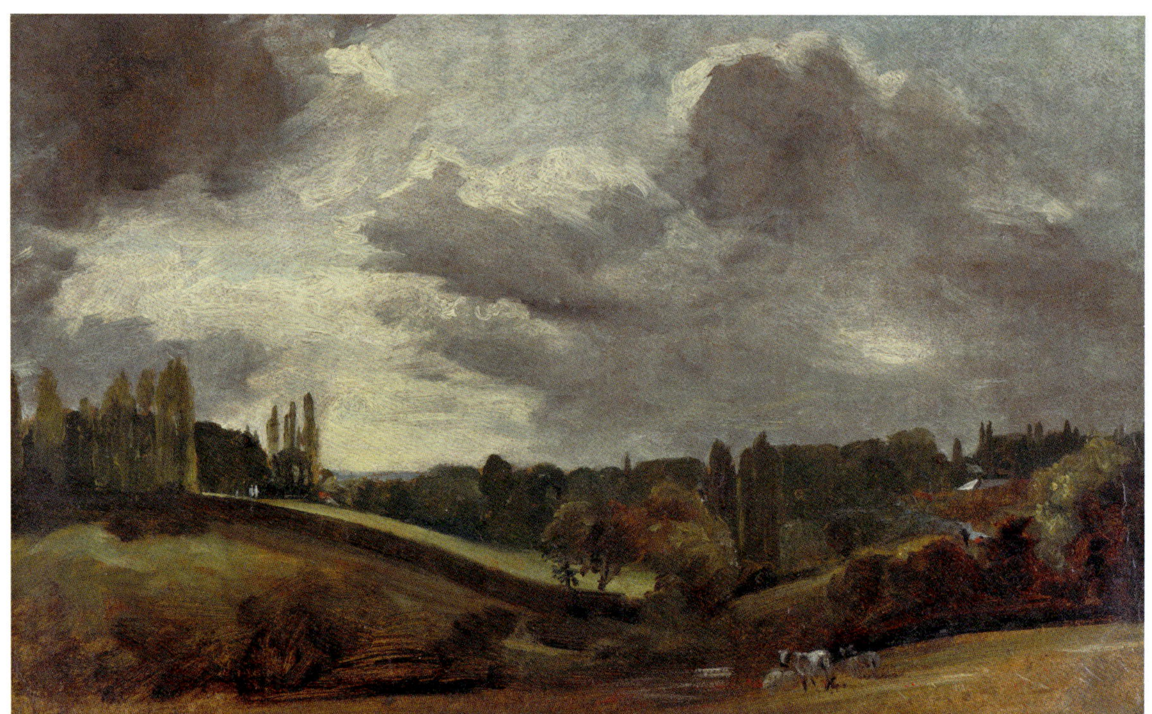

15

14
View towards the Rectory, East Bergholt 1813
oil on canvas, mounted on board, 4¼ × 5⅝ in. (10.8 × 14.3 cm)

15
East Bergholt ca. 1813
oil on board, 12½× 18½ in. (31.8 × 47 cm)

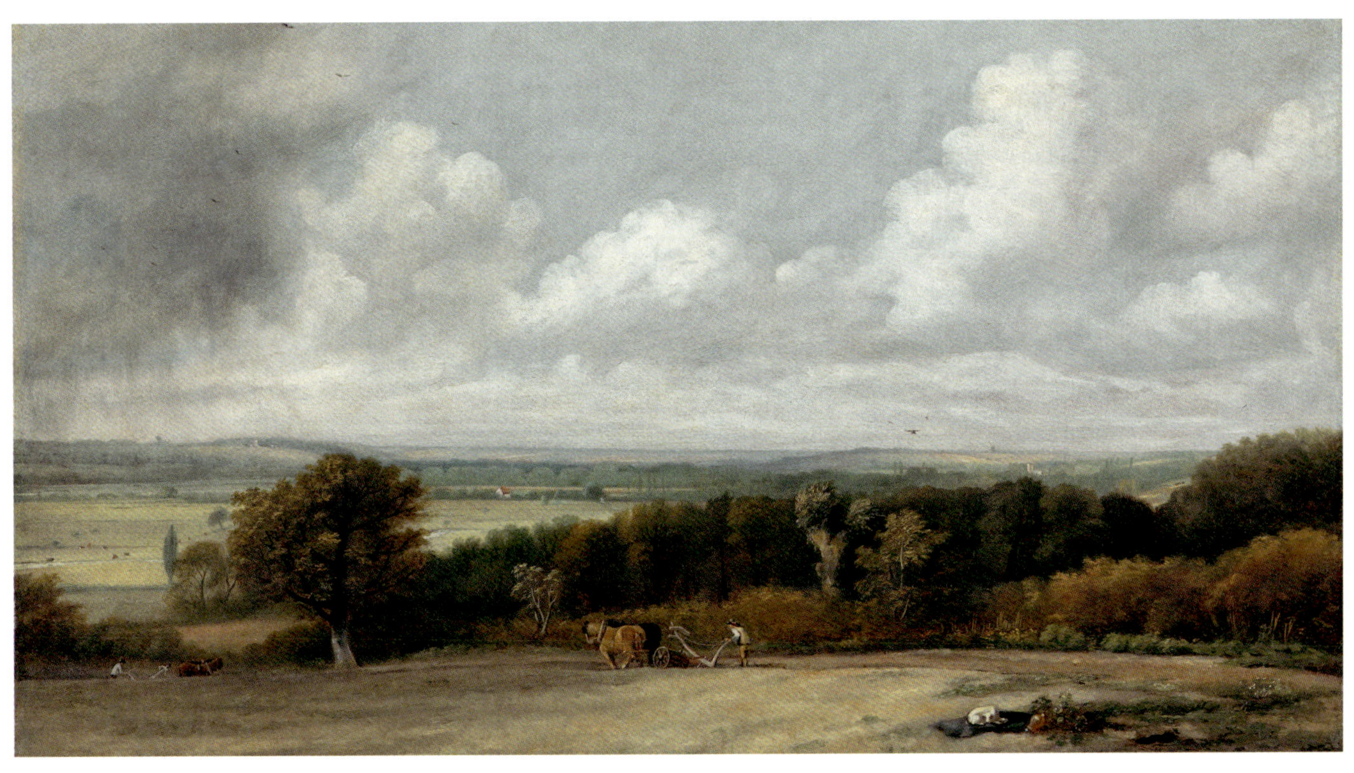

16

16
Ploughing Scene in Suffolk 1824–25
oil on canvas, 16¾ × 30 in. (42.5 × 76.2 cm)

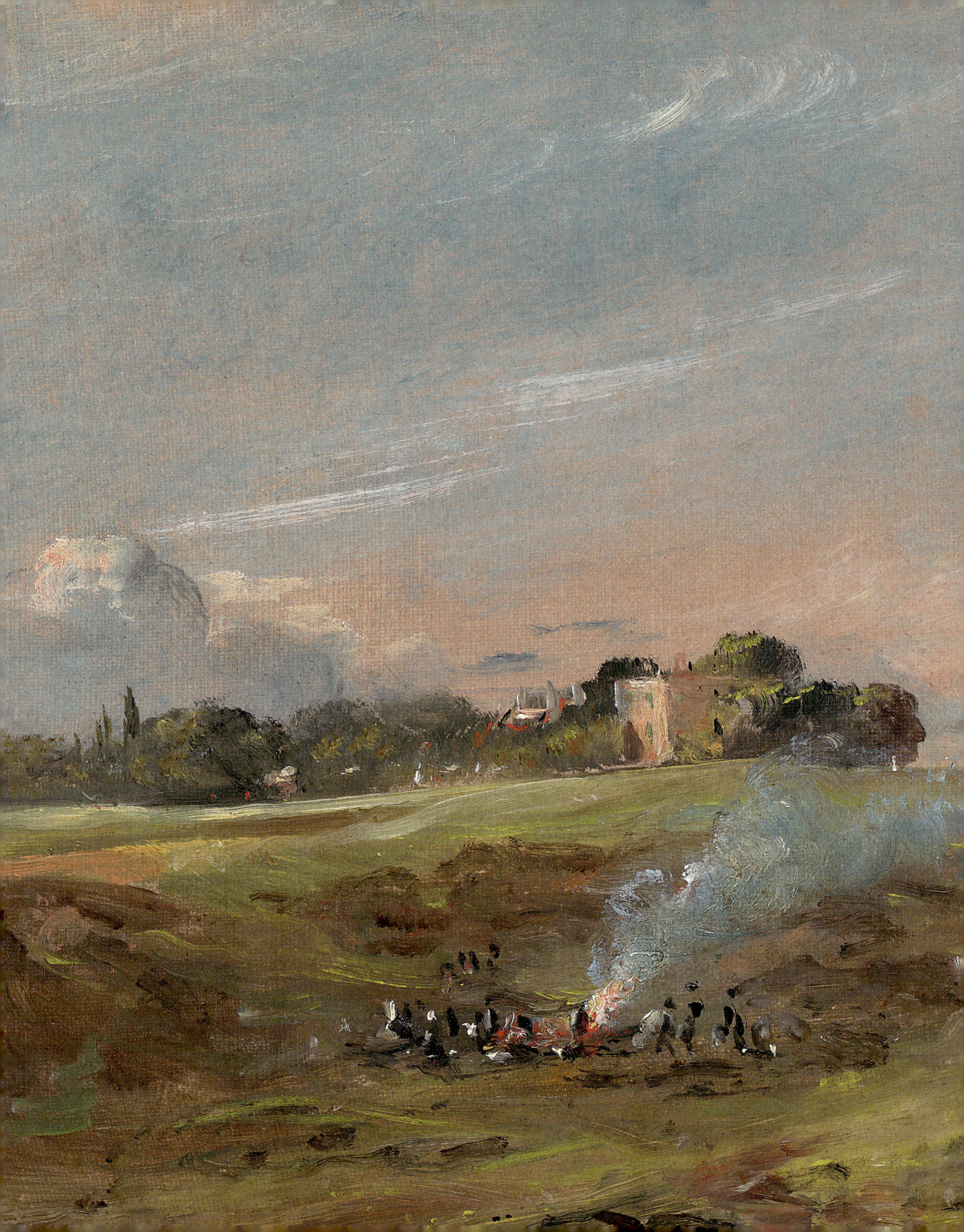

Later Paintings and Oil Sketches

After an extended stay in Suffolk with Maria in late summer 1817, Constable returned only for short visits. This marked a fundamental caesura in his artistic practice. Although he continued to paint subjects from the Stour Valley, he now relied on the archive of sketches and drawings he had accumulated, distilling from them exhibition paintings of extraordinary ambition. "I do not consider myself at work without I am before a six foot canvas," he wrote.

He now made a new kind of small-scale oil sketch in the studio, a compositional study that gave expression to initial ideas for a painting. In these tiny works he took as much care to indicate atmosphere and mood as to block out the main elements of the composition. Despite their modest size, the sketches aspired to design self-consciously artful and dramatic compositions suited to his new status as an associate of the Royal Academy. The small, spirited study for *The Hay Wain* (plate 20) is a fine example: Filled with energy, it can be seen as a key moment in the genesis of Constable's most celebrated composition.

The luminous, six-foot *Stratford Mill* represents Constable's unique practice of making a freely worked sketch the same size as the finished painting (plate 17). Some, such as those for *The Hay Wain* (1821, Victoria and Albert Museum) and *Hadleigh Castle* (ca. 1828–29, Tate Britain), are freer in handling than this, spiraling off in places to mark-making that cannot be linked to a specific referent in nature. The full-scale sketch for *Stratford Mill*, though, pays special attention to the foreground, recalling the "Old rotten Banks, slimy posts, & brickwork" that Constable claimed "made me a painter."

Through the 1820s, Constable continued to make smaller oil paintings, some for exhibition, others for private sale. Many hewed closely to established picturesque formulae, as in *Parham Mill, Gillingham* (plate 23). When Constable heard from Reverend

Hampstead Heath, with a Bonfire ca. 1822 (detail of plate 32)

Fisher in 1825 that the mill at Gillingham had been demolished and replaced by a "new, bright, brick, modern, improved patent monster," he responded gloomily that "there will soon be an end to the picturesque in the kingdom." His father, who invested in new technologies to bolster the productivity of his mills, might have had a different view.

In Hampstead, from 1819 onward, Constable took up outdoor oil sketching with renewed enthusiasm, employing a more extensive color palette than in Suffolk (plates 24, 33). Although the heath offered much in the way of visual incident, Constable struggled to find subject matter for a six-footer. A favored subject for smaller paintings was Branch Hill Pond, where boys swam for recreation while sand was excavated from gravel pits and carted away to support the "march of bricks and mortar" in nearby London. Respectable families enjoyed the sweeping view away from London toward Harrow on a brisk autumn day (plate 30); groups of itinerants or revelers gathered round fires (plate 32). A large, moody oil sketch, probably dating from 1825, may represent the early stages of an unfinished painting of Branch Hill Pond; bereft of incident beyond a single figure and two grazing cows, it captures the somber drama that Constable found in the clouds at Hampstead (plate 34).

The sky studies made at Hampstead (discussed by Nicholas Robbins, pp. 107–19) stand among Constable's consummate achievements. They differ from his earlier sketches, seeming to set aside both topography and questions of personal association and focusing instead on empirical observation. With scientific care, Constable took pains to annotate his oil sketches, noting the exact conditions he had recorded. For example, he wrote on the backing board of one cloud study, "Sept'r 13th one o'clock. Slight wind at North West, which became tempestuous in the afternoon, with rain all the night following" (see p. 108, fig. 1).

Hadleigh Castle, the only exhibited six-footer in the Yale Center for British Art's collection, is an exceptional work (plate 38). Constable's first submission to the Royal Academy after being elected a full member, the painting marked the abandonment of the precise finish applied so rigorously to works like *The Hay Wain* (see p. 13, fig. 4) or *Stratford Mill* (see p. 23, fig. 13). In place of detail, Constable achieved breadth. Although more restrained than that of the truly apocalyptic full-size sketch (see p. 29, fig. 18), the surface of the exhibited painting is flecked with white, added with a vehemence that suggests rage. The staffage are the usual types: shepherd, cowherd, travelers around a fire, a couple walking. But here the figures seem like isolated survivors after a catastrophe. The old social structure seen in *The Wheat Field* of 1816, which embraced every member of village society (see p. 21, fig. 12), has collapsed into modern capitalism's dystopian landscape of isolation and alienation. The painting is an anguished song of experience, demonstrating, to their full compass, the expressive possibilities of landscape painting.

17
Full-Size Sketch for "Stratford Mill" 1819–20
oil on canvas, 51½ × 72½ in. (130.8 × 184.2 cm)
PAUL MELLON FUND

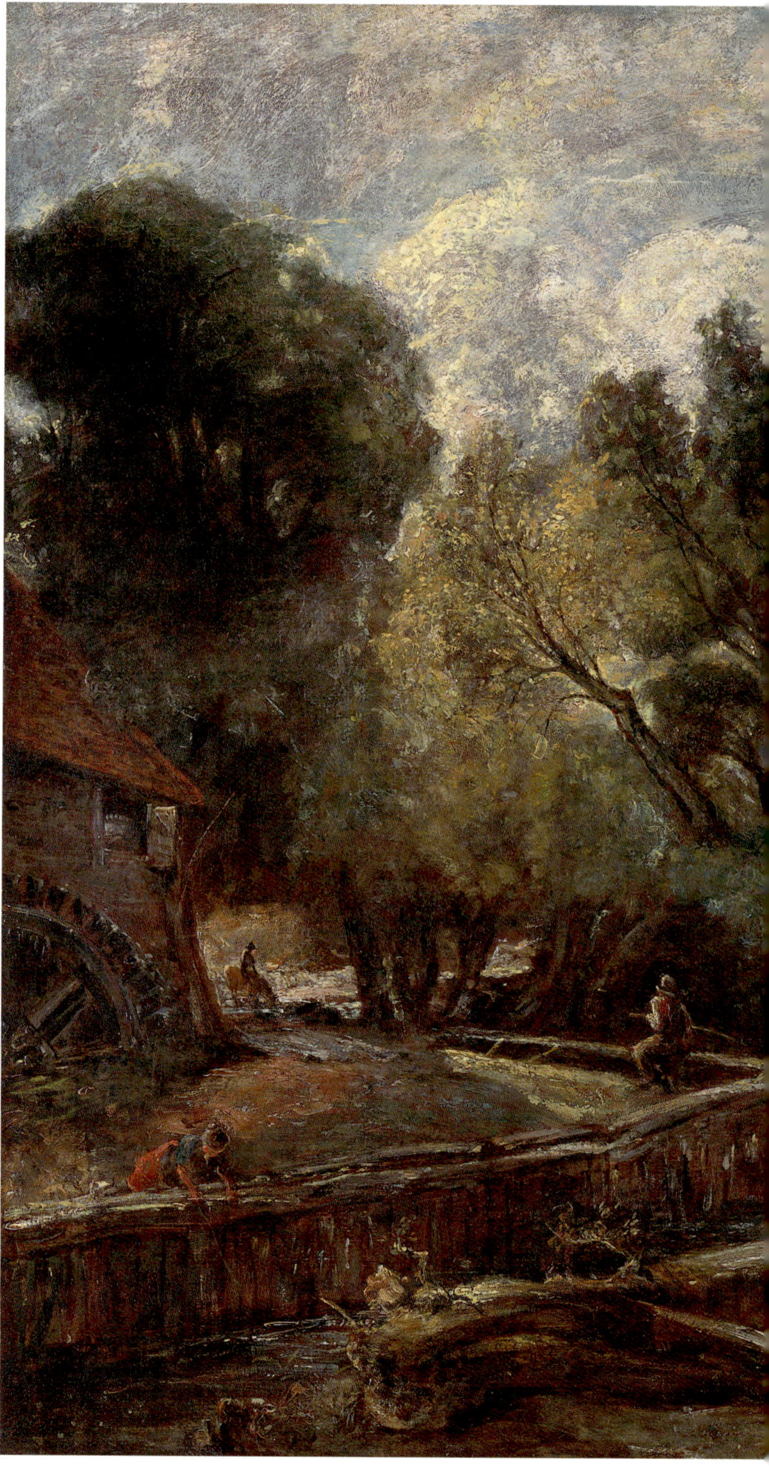

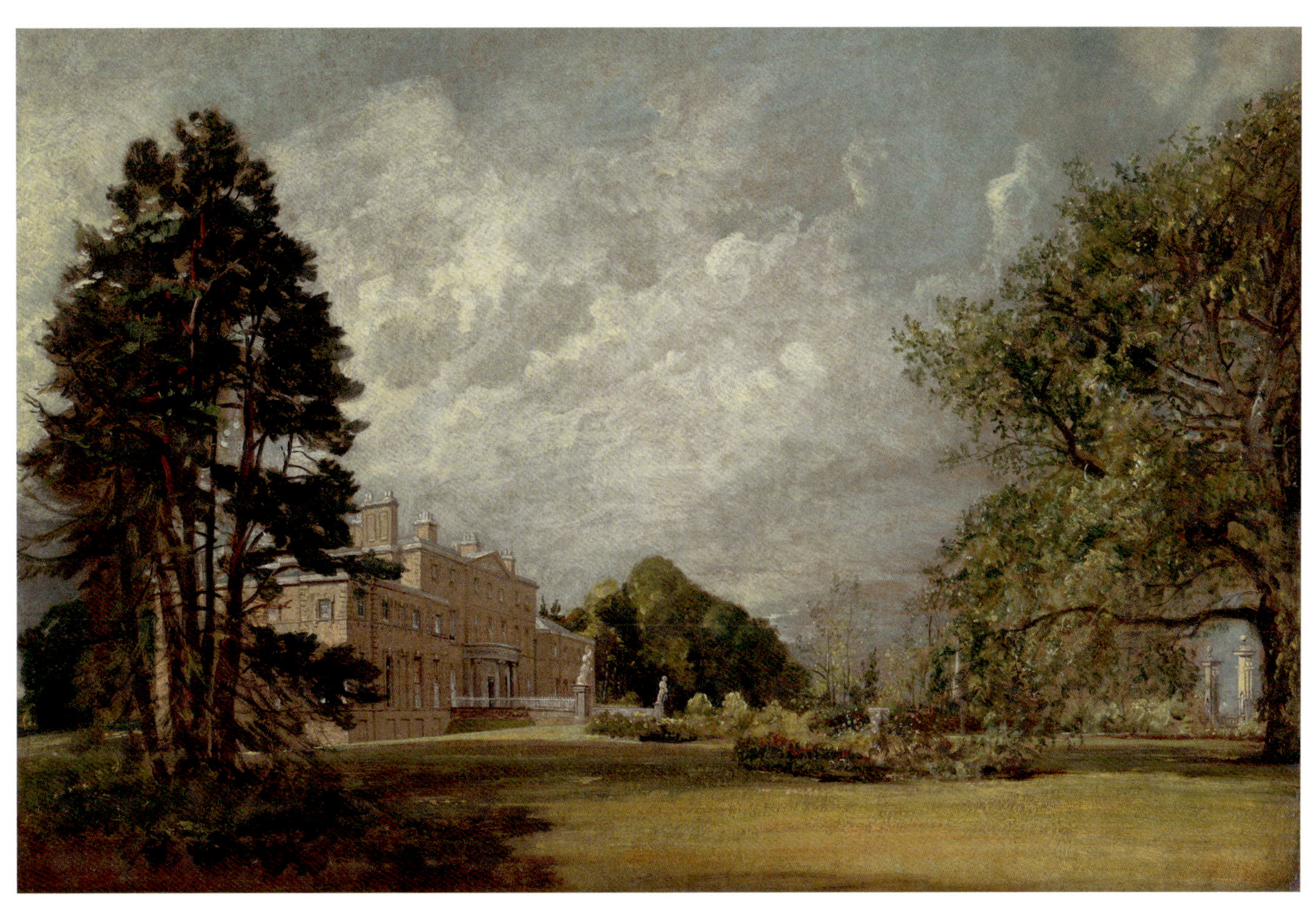

22

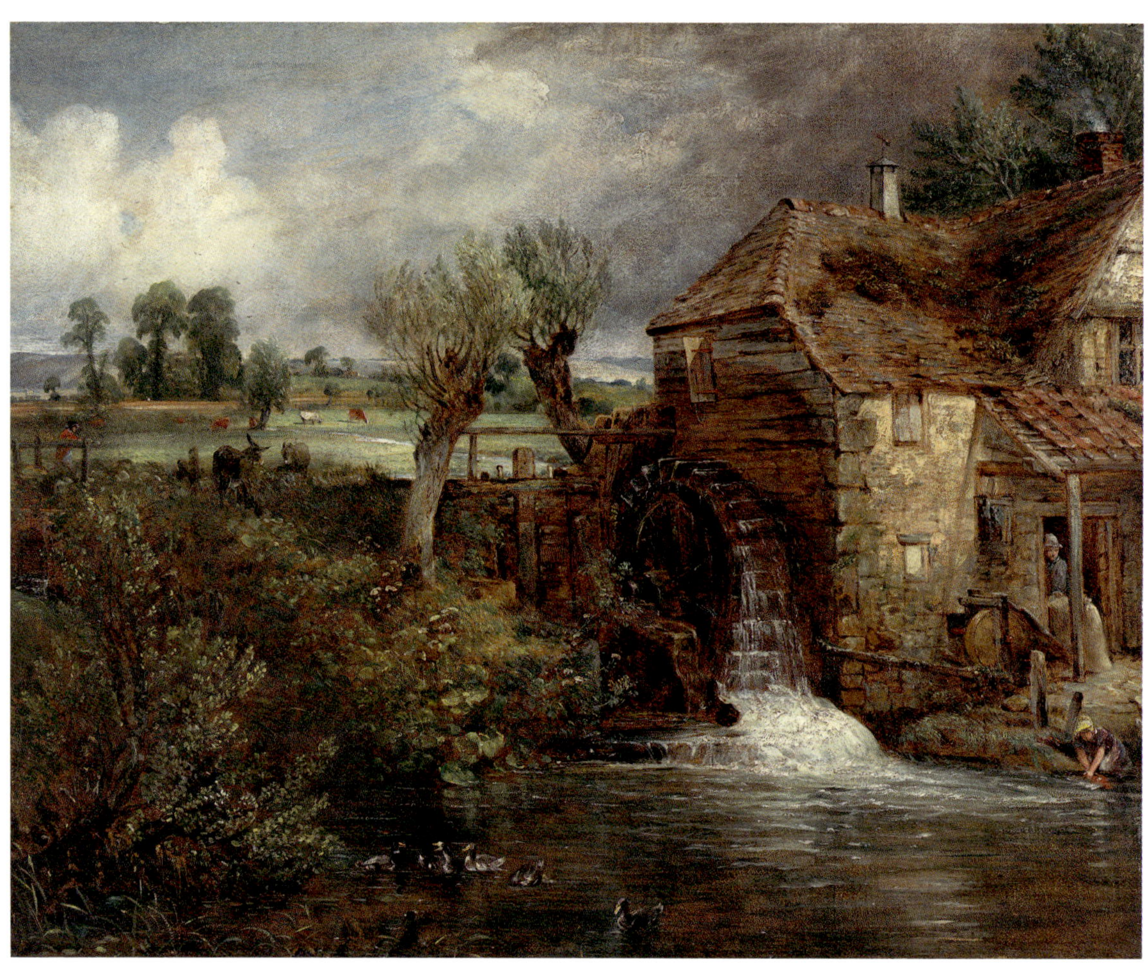

23

23

Parham Mill, Gillingham ca. 1826
oil on canvas, 19¾ × 23¾ in. (50.2 × 60.3 cm)

24

Hampstead Heath 1820–30
oil on canvas, 17¾ × 14 in. (45.1 × 35.6 cm)
PAUL MELLON FUND

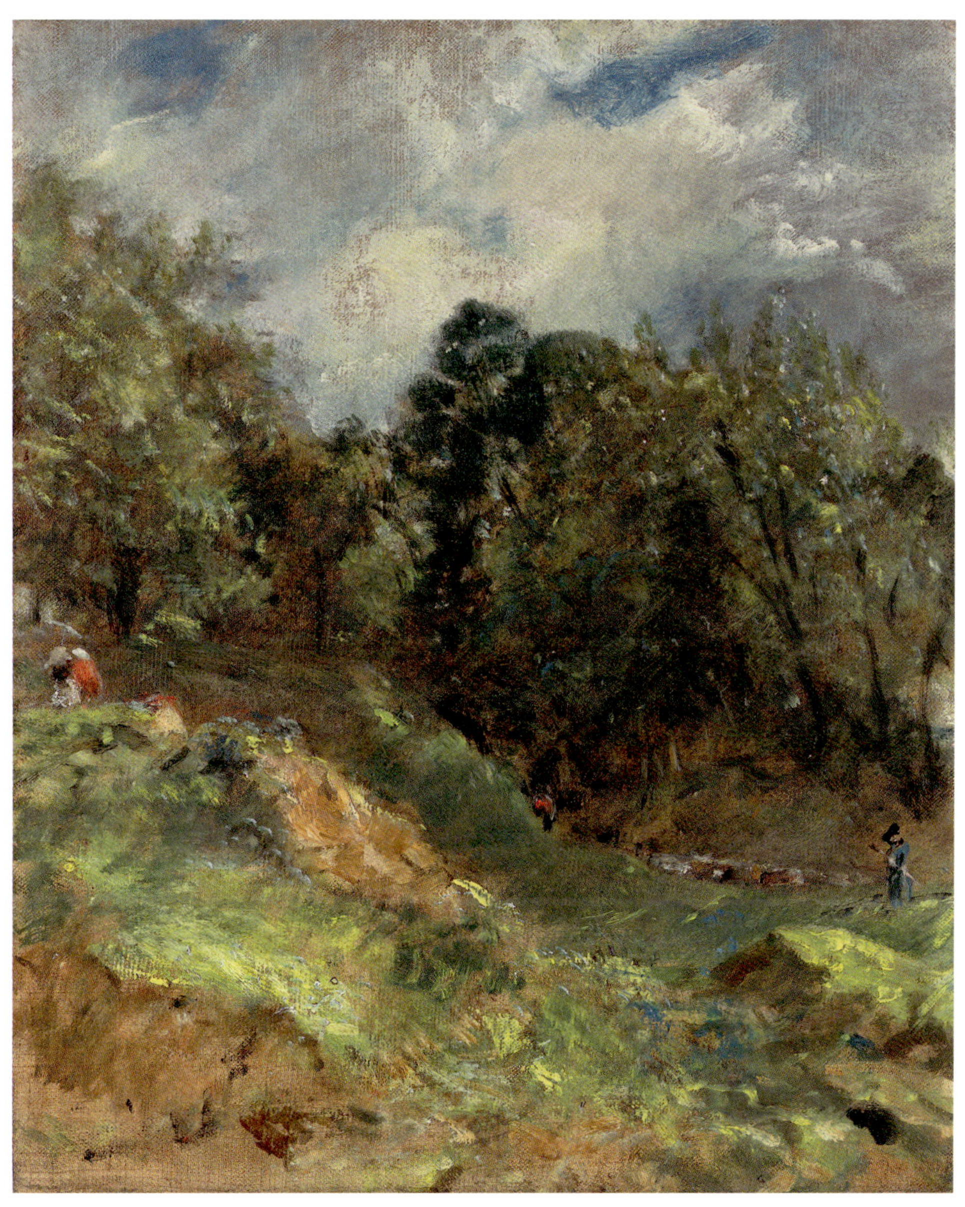

24

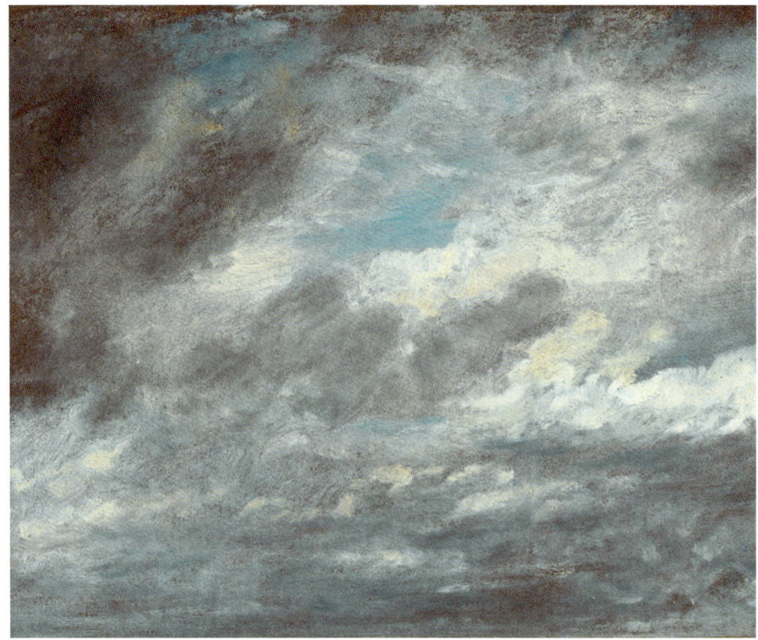

25

26

25
Cloud Study ca. 1821
oil on paper, mounted on card,
9⅜ × 11½ in. (23.8 × 29.2 cm)

26
Cloud Study 1821
oil on paper, mounted on panel,
8⅜ × 11½ in. (21.3 × 29.2 cm)

27
Cloud Study 1822
oil on paper, mounted on panel,
11¼ × 19 in. (28.6 × 48.3 cm)

28
Cloud Study 1822
oil on paper, mounted on canvas,
12 × 20 in. (30.5 × 50.8 cm)

27

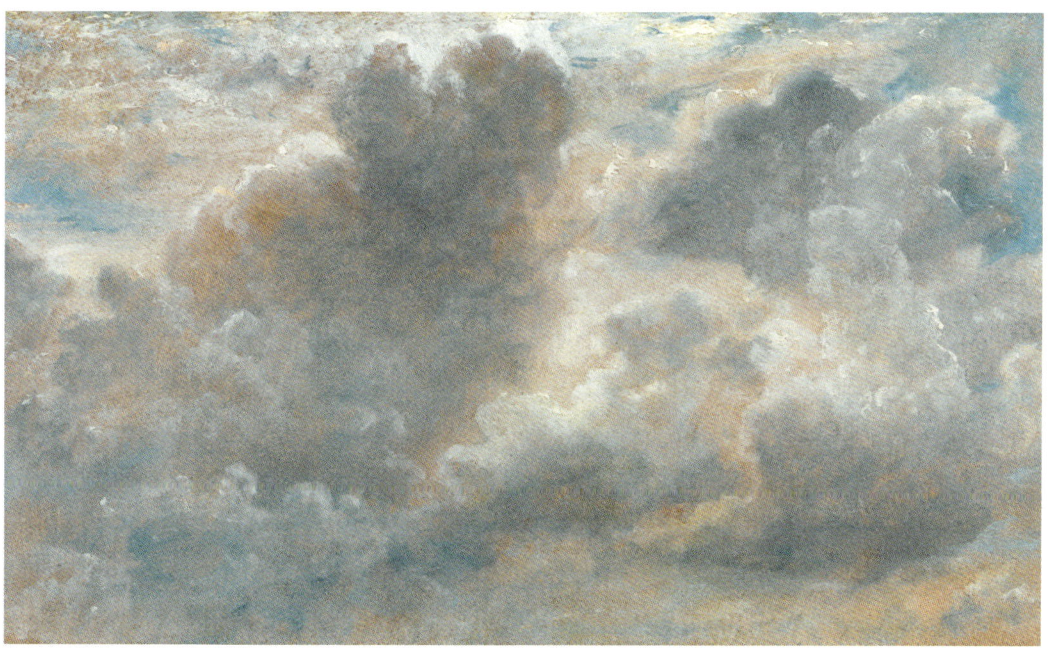

28

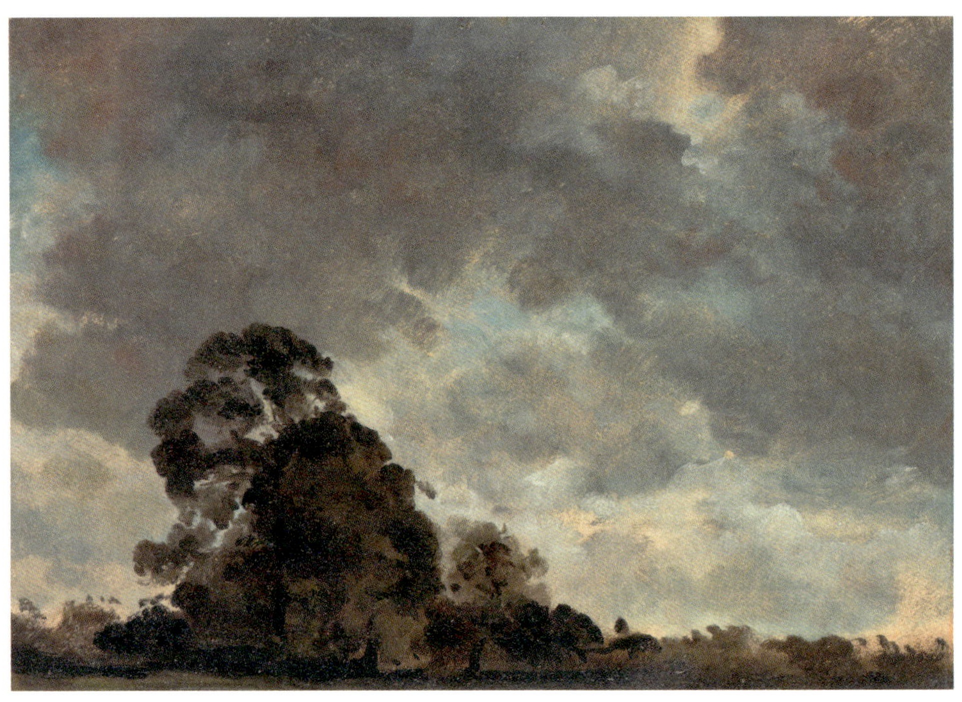

29

29

Cloud Study ca. 1821
oil on paper, mounted on card, 8 × 10¾ in. (20.3 × 27.3 cm)

30

Hampstead Heath Looking towards Harrow 1821
oil on paper, mounted on canvas, 10⅜ × 12¼ in. (26.4 × 31.1 cm)

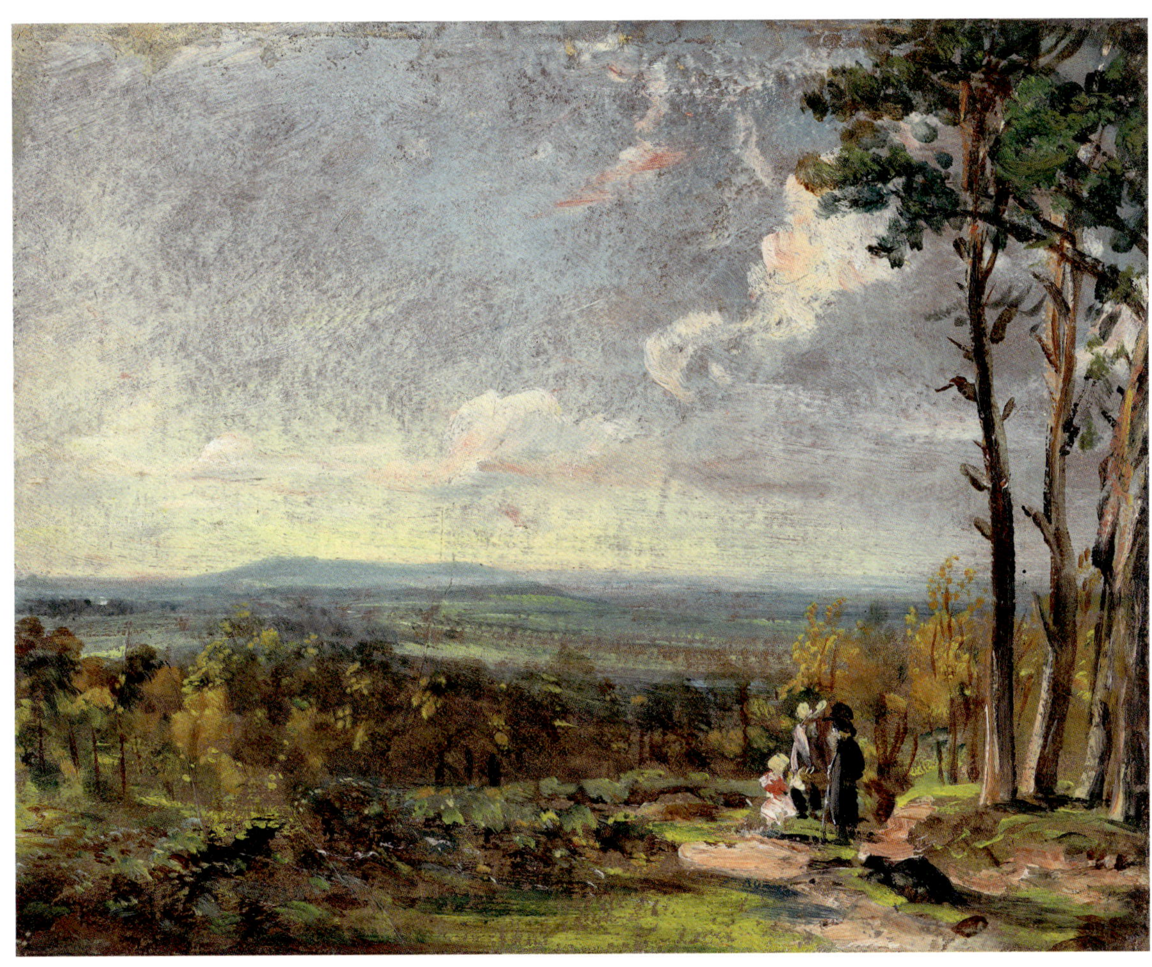

30

31
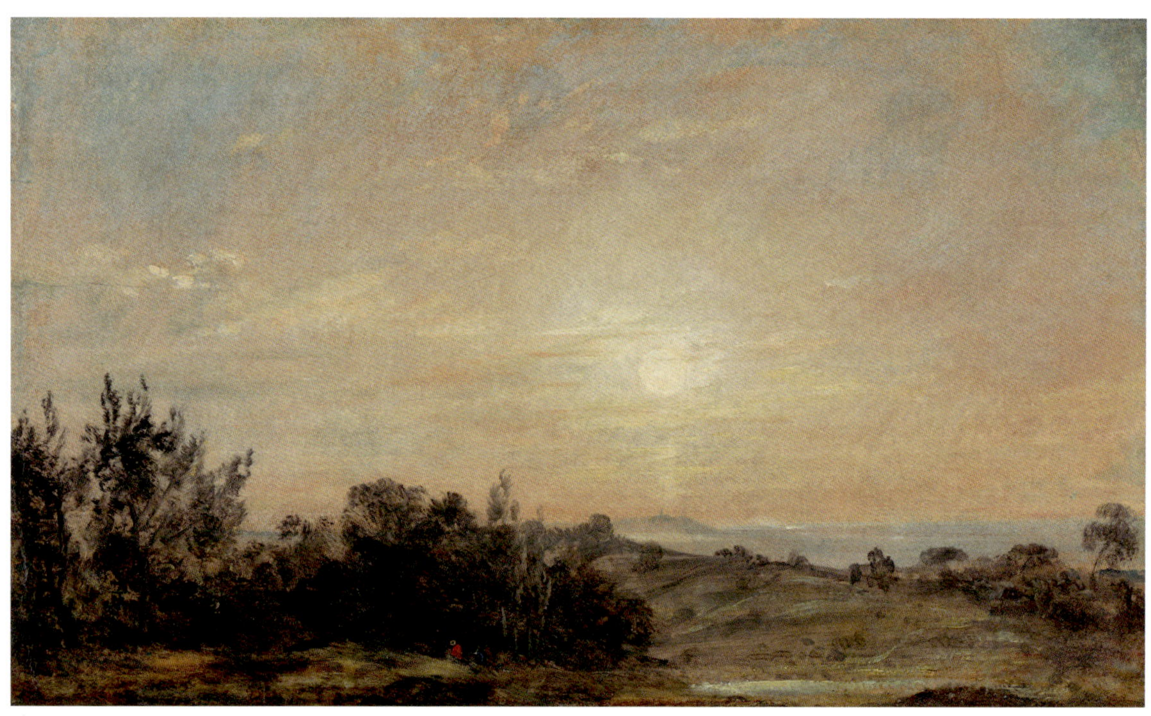

31
Hampstead Heath Looking towards Harrow 1821–22
oil on paper, mounted on canvas, 11⅝ × 19 in. (29.5 × 48.3 cm)

32
Hampstead Heath, with a Bonfire ca. 1822
oil on canvas, 10⅝ × 12⅝ in. (27 × 32.1 cm)

33
A View at Hampstead with Stormy Weather ca. 1830
oil on paper, mounted on panel, 6⅛ × 7⅝ in. (15.6 × 19.4 cm)

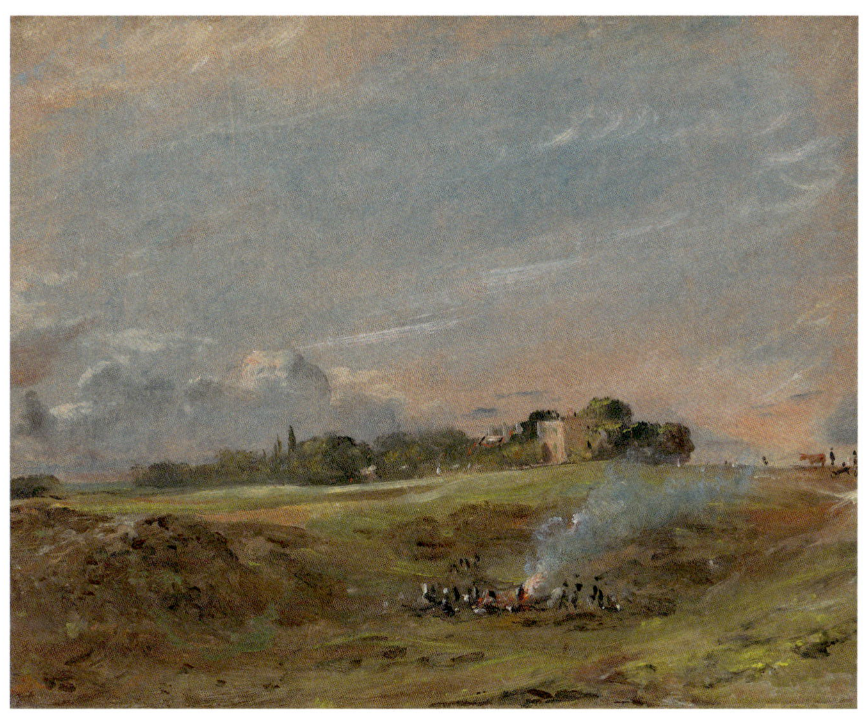

32

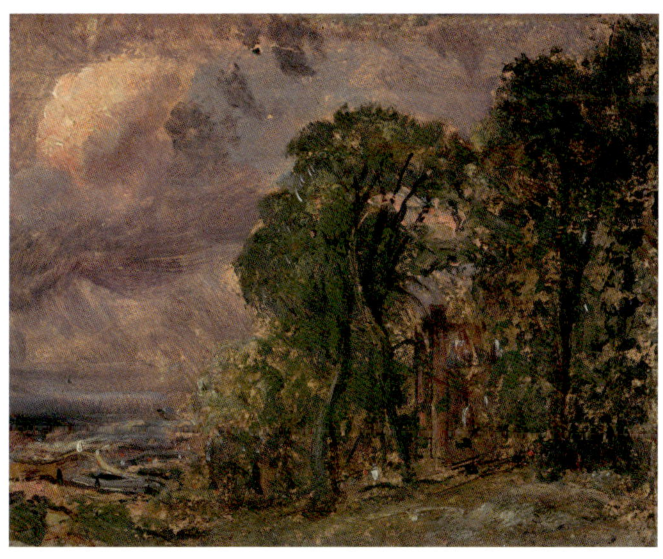

33

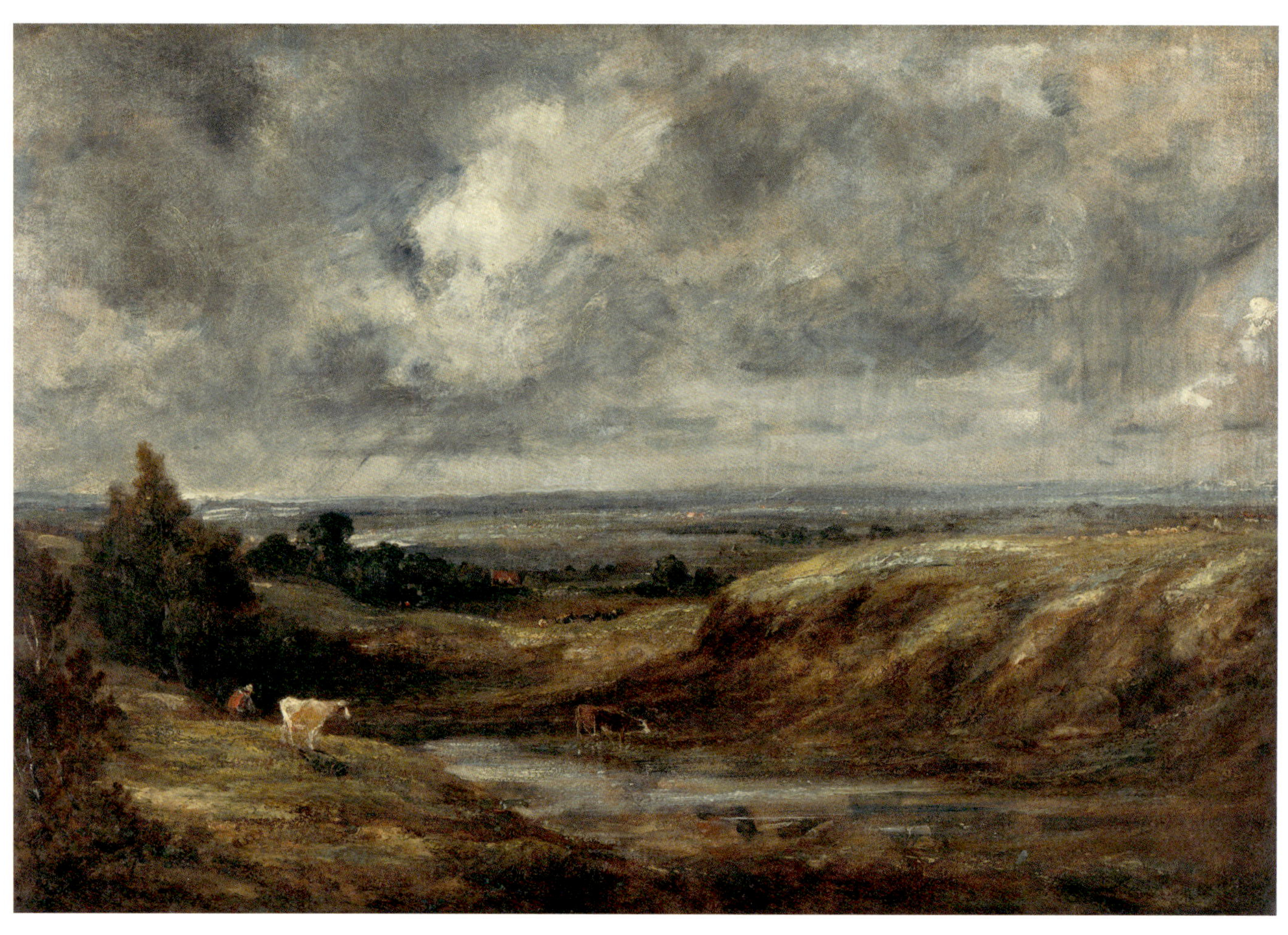

34

34
Hampstead Heath ca. 1825
oil on canvas, 18 × 25½ in. (45.7 × 64.8 cm)

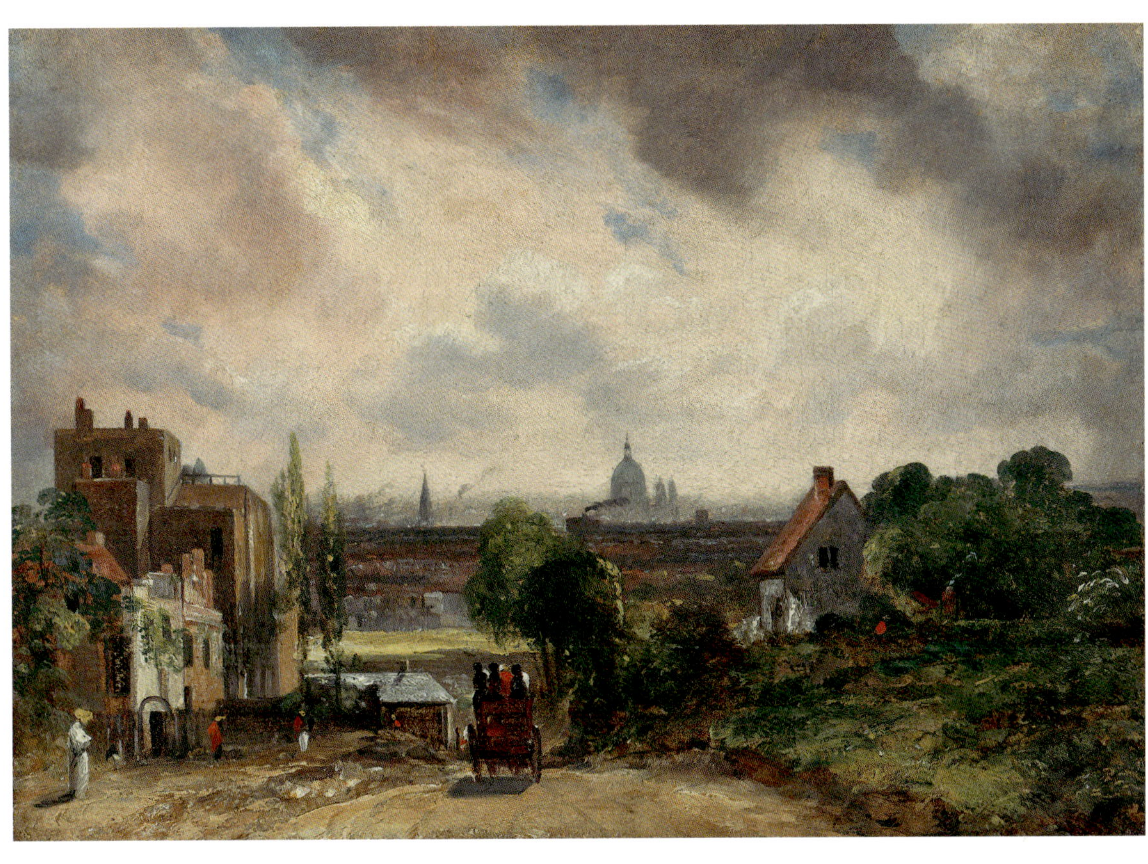

35

35
Sir Richard Steele's Cottage, Hampstead 1831–32
oil on canvas, 8¼ × 11¼ in. (21 × 28.6 cm)

36

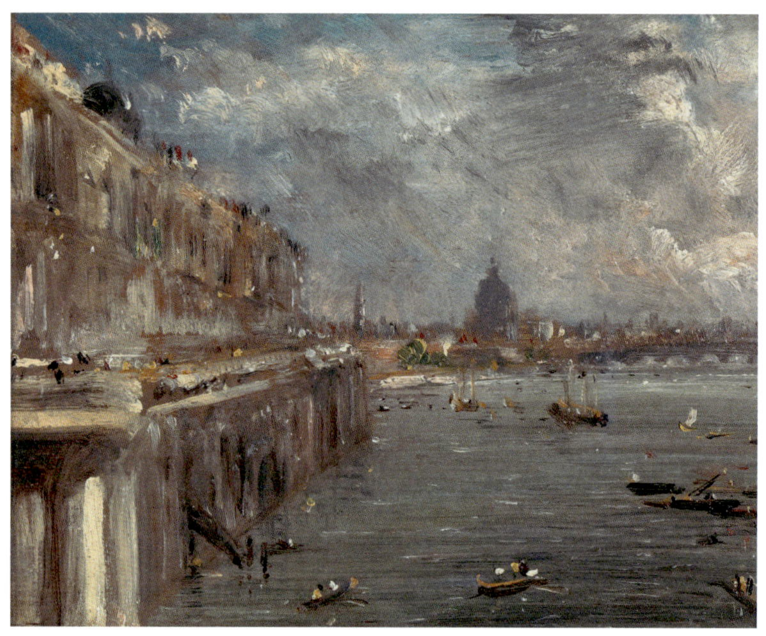

36
Somerset House Terrace from Waterloo Bridge ca. 1819
oil on panel, 6⅛ × 7⅜ in. (15.6 × 18.7 cm)

37
Half-Size Sketch for "The Opening of Waterloo Bridge ('Whitehall Stairs, June 18, 1817')" 1829–31
oil on canvas, 24 × 39 in. (61 × 99.1 cm)

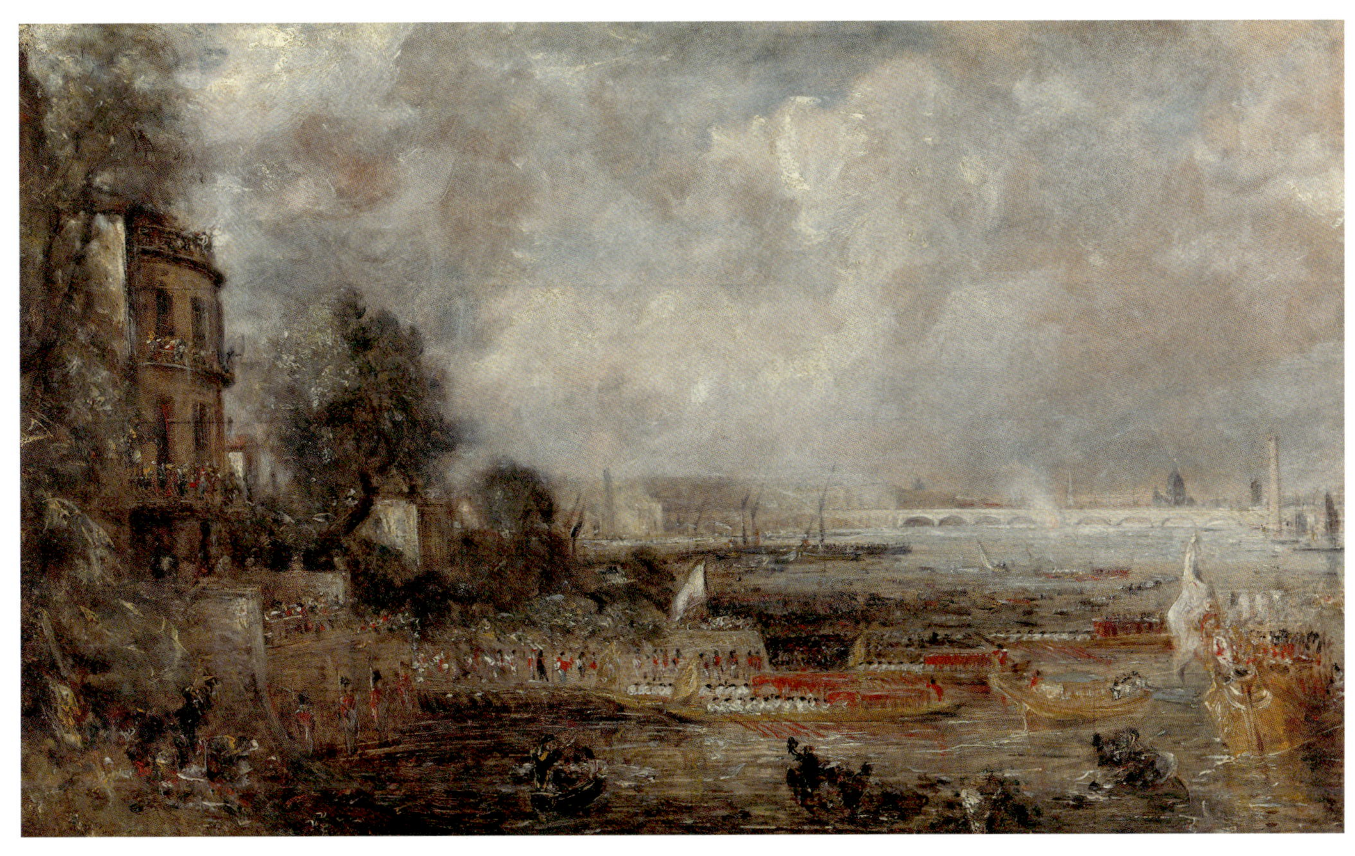

37

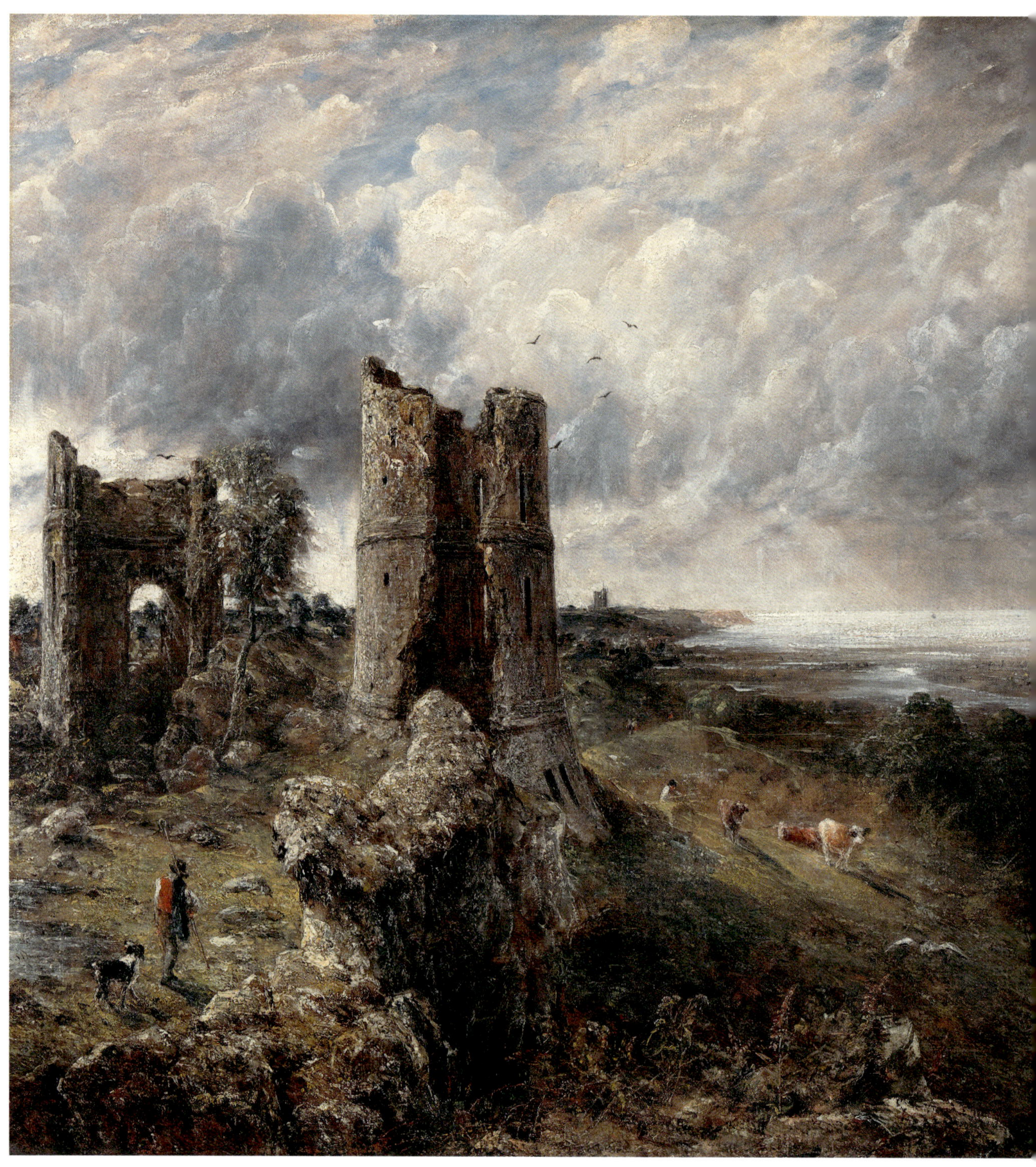

38

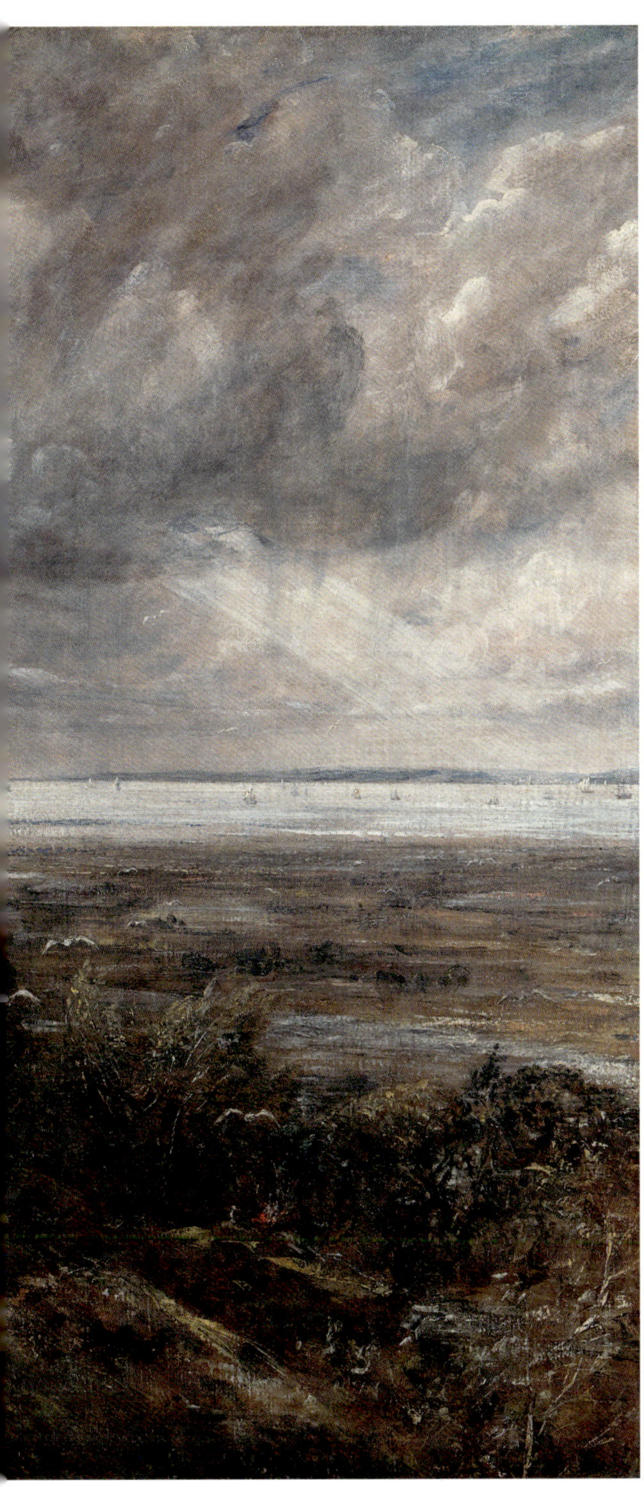

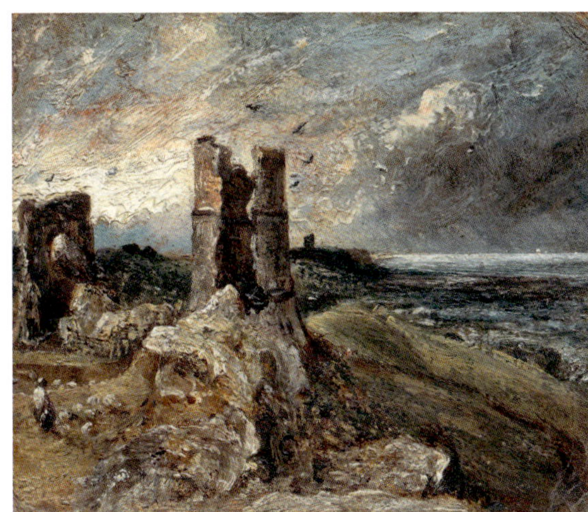

39

38
Hadleigh Castle, The Mouth of the Thames—Morning after a Stormy Night 1829
oil on canvas, 48 × 64¾ in. (121.9 × 164.5 cm)

39
Hadleigh Castle 1828–29
oil on millboard, 7⅞ × 9½ in. (20 × 24 cm)

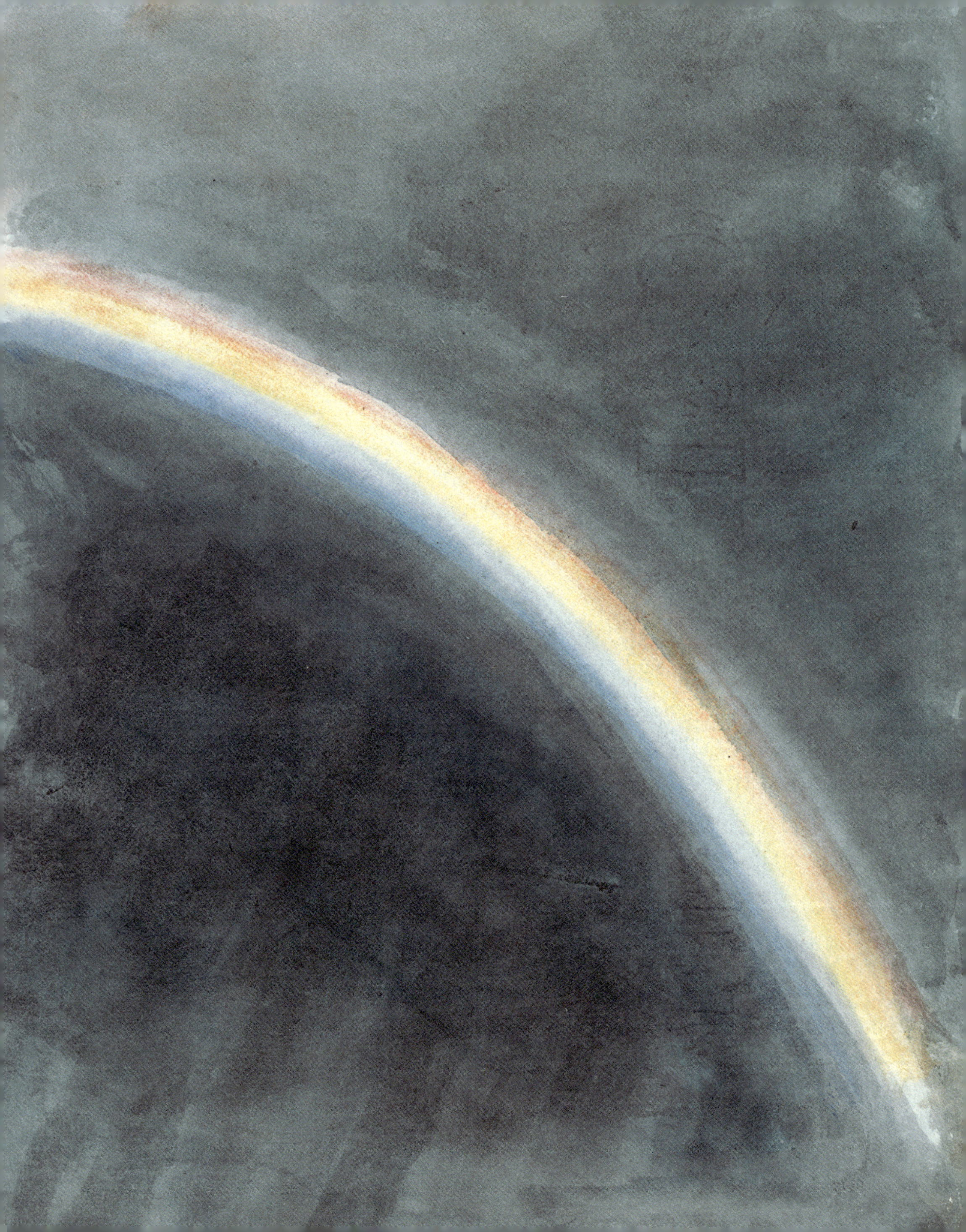

Drawings and Watercolors

Although Constable's reputation rests largely on his oil paintings, his drawings and watercolors form a significant body of work. In eighteenth-century Britain, drawing took many forms. It was an acceptable form of artistic practice for the gentleman amateur and a genteel accomplishment for women of the leisure classes. Artists such as Joshua Reynolds (1723–1792) and Thomas Lawrence (1769–1830), skilled draftsmen themselves, collected old master drawings, which they believed best revealed the artist's genius. Drawing from the antique and the life model was foundational to the professional training of an academic artist such as Constable (plate 47). For the landscape painter, sketching from nature in pencil or watercolor was an essential practice, a more or less mandatory preparatory stage in the creation of a painting.

Drawing was a constant activity throughout Constable's career. His earliest works on paper are timid and formulaic, but some contain hints of his artistic ambition. *Cottage among Trees*, dating from the mid-1790s, is a conventional exercise in the picturesque, timidly executed in graphite and gray wash (plate 40). It may reflect the influence of John Thomas Smith, who admired tumbledown cottages in his publication *Remarks on Rural Scenery*, from 1797. Smith also recommended penetrating "into the inmost recesses of forests" for subject matter, and, while drawing at Helmingham Park in 1800, Constable found himself "quite alone among the Oaks and solitude." He was enchanted by the outlines of the ancient trees and returned decades later to a drawing made at Helmingham (plate 41), which lies in the ancestry of a series of elegiac oil compositions, one of which was engraved for *English Landscape* (plate 64).

Maturing as an artist, Constable experimented with bolder compositions. *Trees in a Meadow*, dating to around 1805, sees him using graphite and chalk to lay out a composition that acquires a sense of mass through the application of watercolor (plate 44).

Sky Study with Rainbow 1827 (plate 57)

His sensitivity to lighting conditions, a keynote of later works, is apparent in *Landscape at East Bergholt*, circa 1805, where light washes of color conjure a sense of clouds moving behind the boughs of a tree in full leaf (plate 43). More confident in execution is the emphatic *Wooded Slope with a Receding Road,* where trees take on sculptural heft in a landscape whose perspectival recession is heightened with strongly contrasted areas of dark and light (plate 45).

In 1806 Constable spent seven weeks in the Lake District, whose fame as a sketching ground was well established in the work of artists like Francis Towne, Edward Dayes, and, after 1797, Turner. A significant technical exemplar for the young Constable was Dayes's student Thomas Girtin (1775–1802), the watercolor painter who had died young only four years earlier, and whose work was much admired by Constable's mentor George Beaumont. Beaumont had been to the Lakes himself and commissioned Girtin to work up into finished watercolors sketches the amateur had made there. Constable saw these hybrid works before setting off for the north. *Borrowdale: Evening after a Fine Day, 1 October 1806* shares Girtin's taste for broad, sweeping compositions unadorned with picturesque detail (plate 46). Skillfully though Constable responded to the mountainous terrain, it was clear that he was temperamentally at odds with the dramatic, barren scenery that had inspired Turner and Girtin.

Throughout the remainder of his career, Constable used pencil as a medium for exploring compositional possibilities of a subject. *Two Studies of Dedham Church from the East*, made between 1806 and 1808, for example, negotiate with the compositional formula developed by Claude (plate 48). As late as 1825, Constable prepared a sensitive copy of Claude's drawing *Trees and Deer,* owned by Lawrence, carefully emulating its delicate penmanship (plate 52).

Constable's mastery with the pencil is evident in a drawing of the Thames made in the summer, probably around 1818. On the lower reaches of the river, downstream from London Bridge, he observed the busy shipping lane at an obtuse angle from the shore, with smaller vessels aground. A triumphant exercise in perspective, with foreground motifs firmly delineated, graphite digging hard into the paper, the drawing also captures the evanescent effects of sunlight through moving clouds and its reflection on the water (plate 50).

At Salisbury in 1829, Constable made a memorable series of drawings, some in pencil, such as *Salisbury Plain from Old Sarum* (plate 55), others in watercolor. The YCBA pencil drawing *Salisbury Cathedral from the Meadows* (plate 54) belongs in the lineage of the great oil with the same title. Although the work exhibited in 1831 was largely based on a different sketch, made from closer to the cathedral (*Salisbury Cathedral from the North West*, 1829, Fitzwilliam Museum), two crucial elements from the Yale drawing were absorbed into the final composition: the horse-drawn cart to the left, and the slender, pollarded osier tree that, rising from the river bank, breaks the horizon at the right margin of the painting.

Late in his career, influenced perhaps by working with David Lucas on the *English Landscape* mezzotints, Constable used pen and ink to create intensely dramatic tonal images such as the tiny, visionary drawing *Dawn* (plate 53). This miraculous little image compresses onto a sheet of paper smaller than a human hand a dark foreground, stormy sky, landscape, and church spire—the very components of *Salisbury Cathedral from the Meadows*—suggesting the drama of life, death, and redemption.

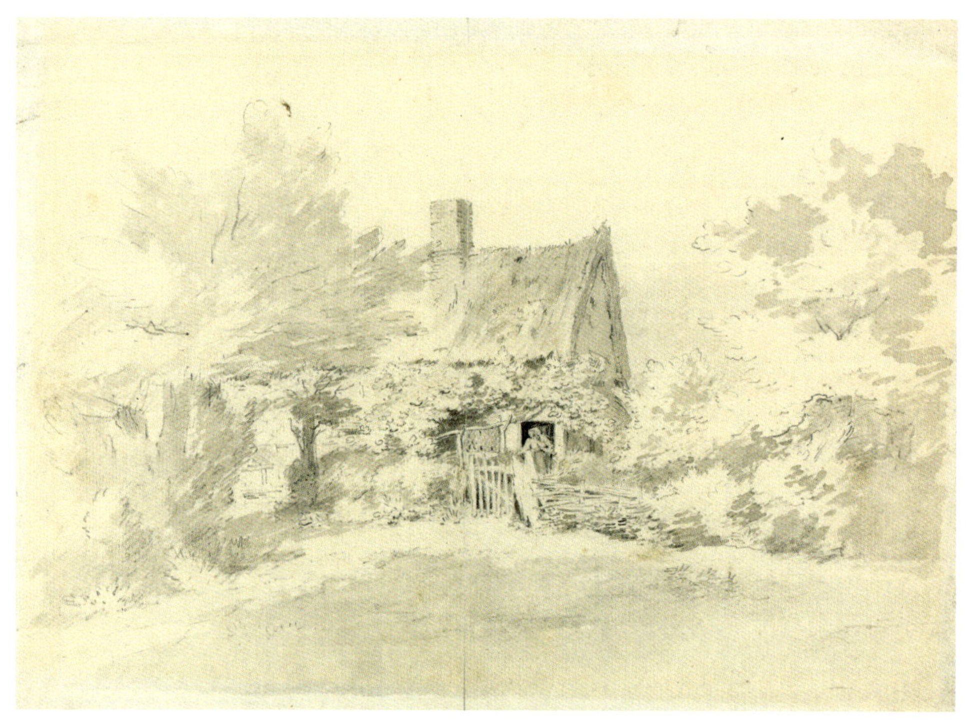
40

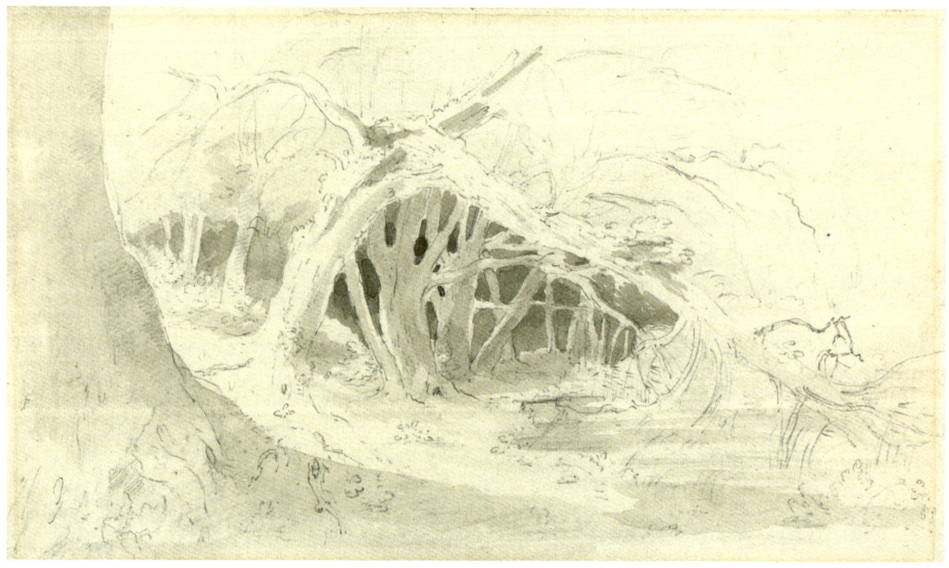
41

40
Cottage among Trees ca. 1795
graphite and gray wash, 11⅜ × 14⅜ in. (28.9 × 36.5 cm)

41
Helmingham: The Silent Pool ca. 1800
graphite and gray wash, 7⅛ × 11⅞ in. (18.1 × 30.2 cm)

42
A Country Girl in the Lake District 1806
watercolor and graphite, 6¾ × 2¾ in. (17.1 × 7 cm)

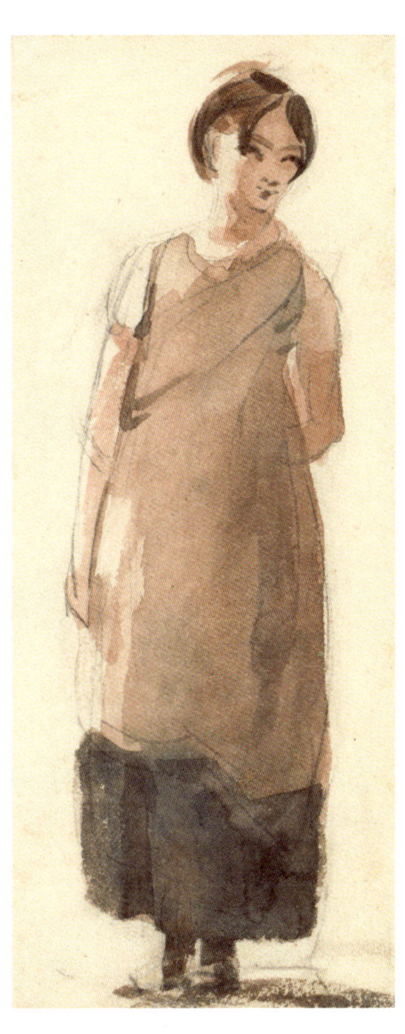
42

43
Landscape at East Bergholt ca. 1805
watercolor and graphite, 7 × 8½ in. (17.8 × 21.6 cm)

44
Trees in a Meadow ca. 1805
watercolor, graphite, and black chalk, 11⅝ × 9⅞ in. (29.5 × 25.1 cm)

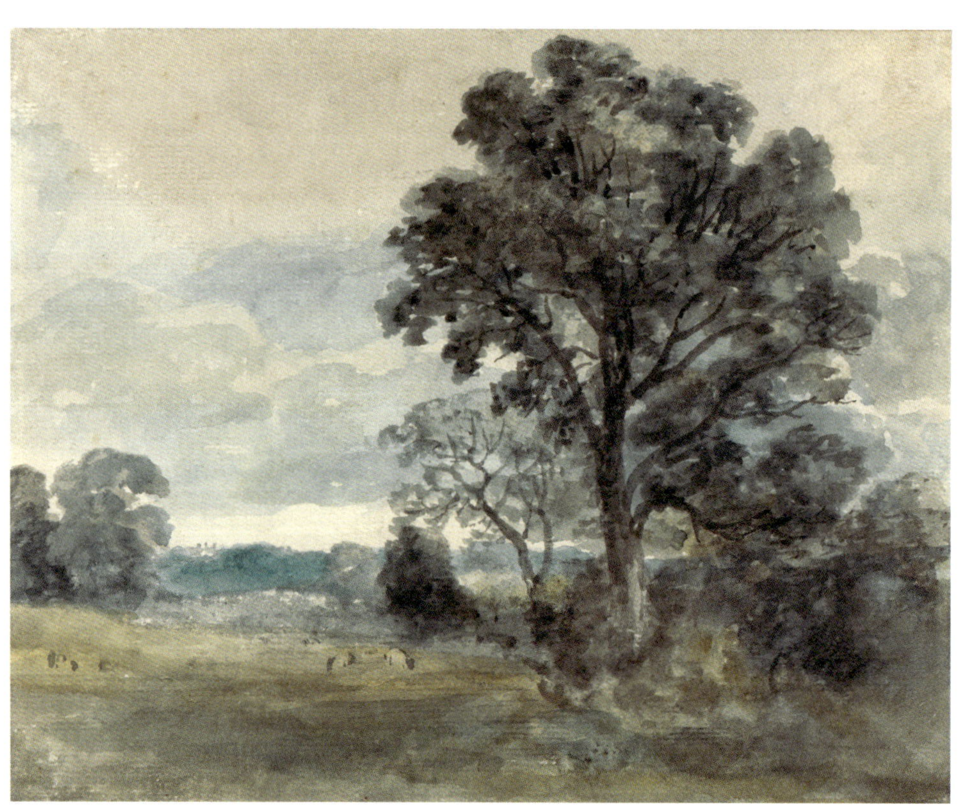

43

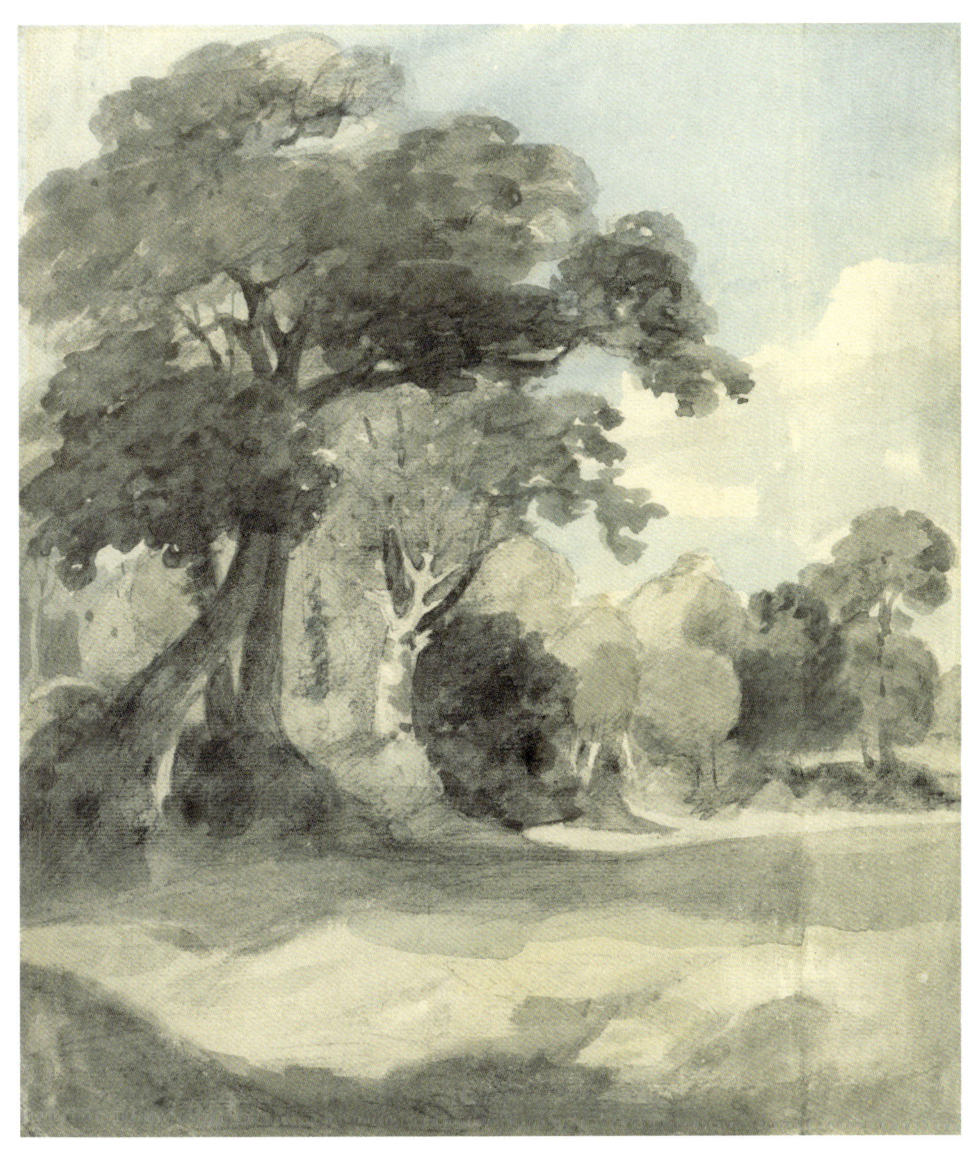

44

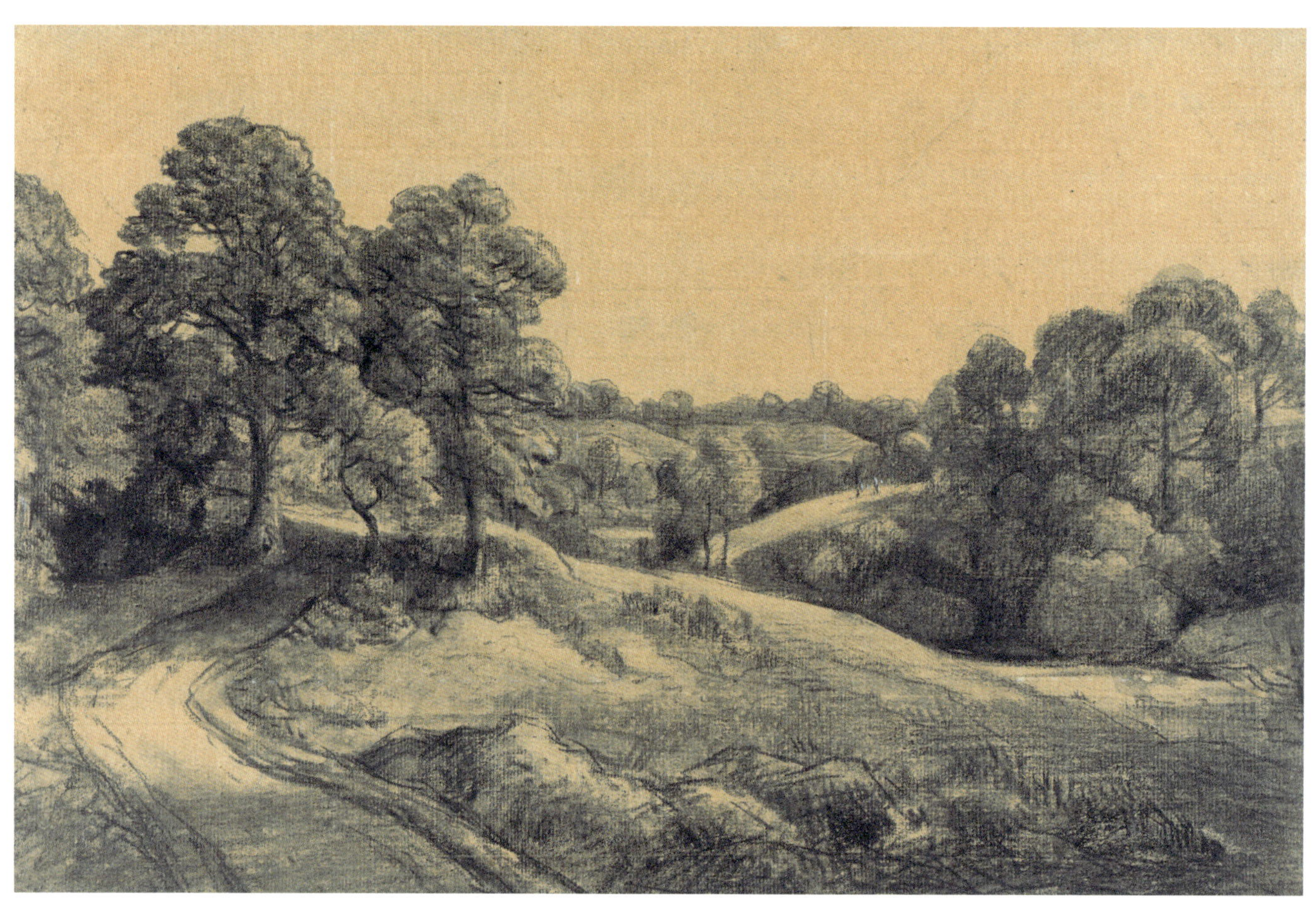

45

45

Wooded Slope with a Receding Road ca. 1805

black chalk with touches of white chalk, 13⅝ × 20⅛ in. (34.6 × 51.1 cm)

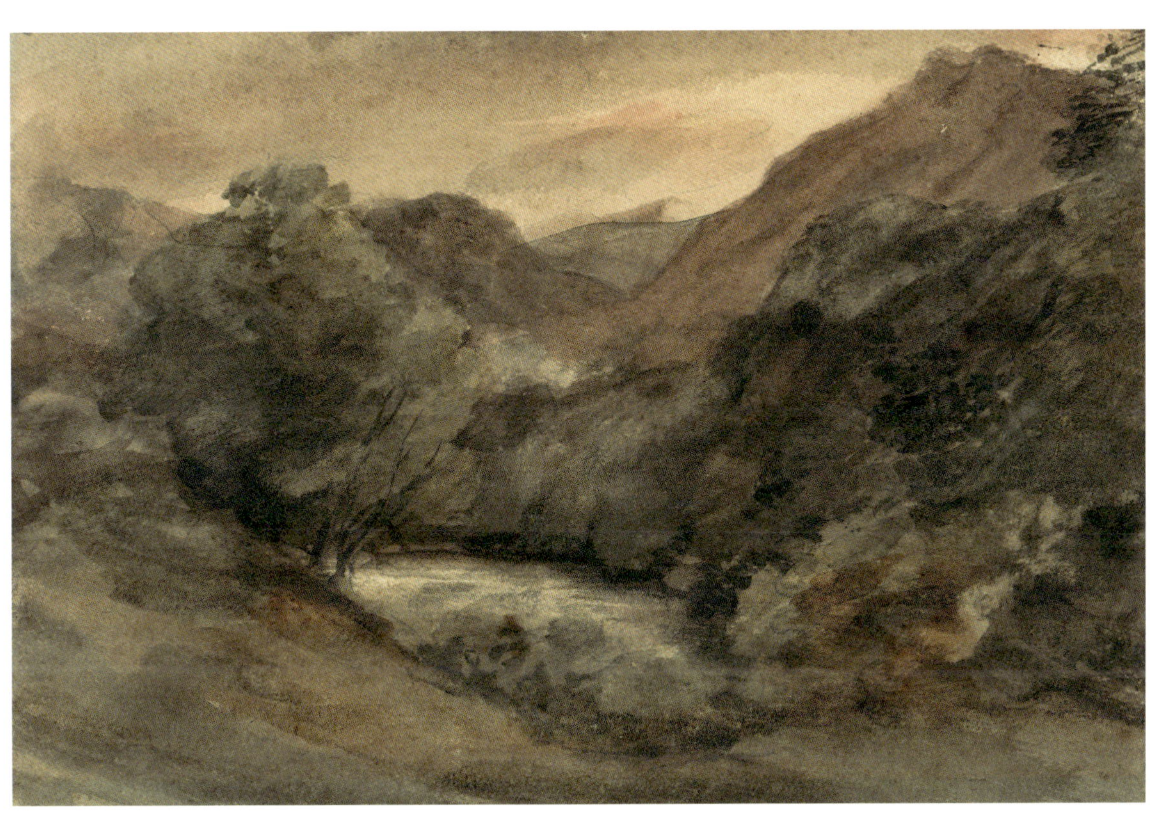

46

46
Borrowdale: Evening after a Fine Day, 1 October 1806 1806
watercolor and graphite with scratching out, 7 × 10½ in. (17.8 × 26.7 cm)

47

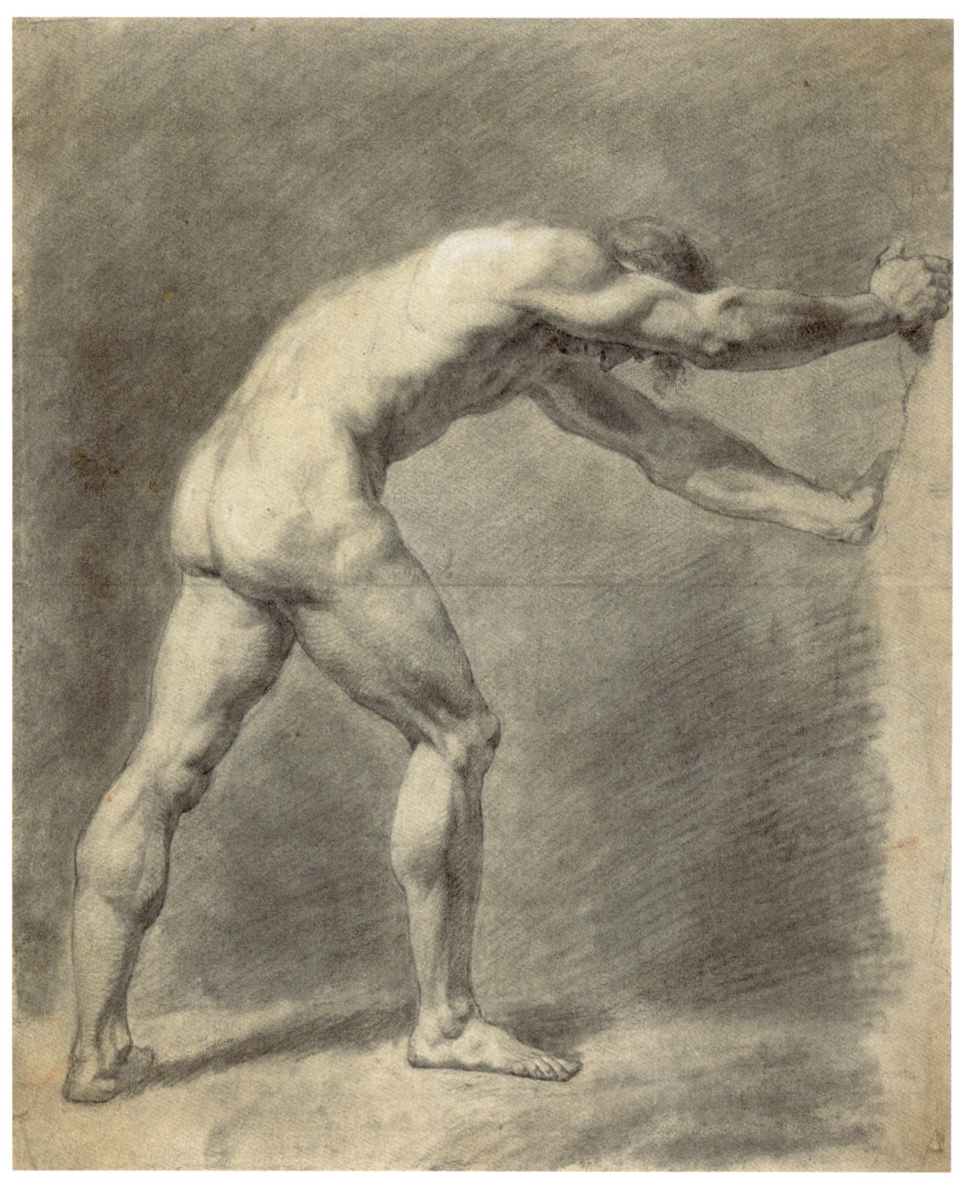

47
Male Nude 1808
graphite and white chalk, 21¾ × 17½ in. (55.2 × 44.5 cm)
PAUL MELLON FUND

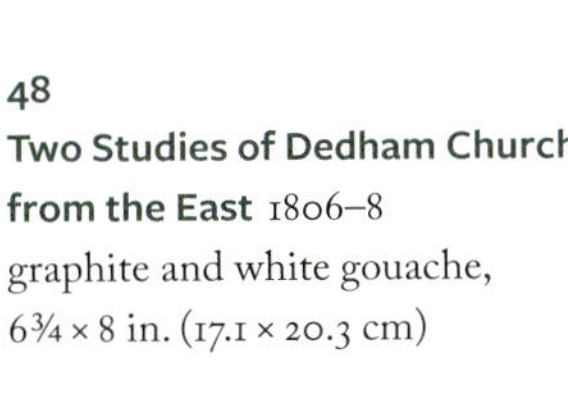

48
Two Studies of Dedham Church from the East 1806–8
graphite and white gouache,
6¾ × 8 in. (17.1 × 20.3 cm)

49
Dedham Vale from Langham ca. 1813
graphite, 7⅛ × 11⅜ in. (18.1 × 28.9 cm)

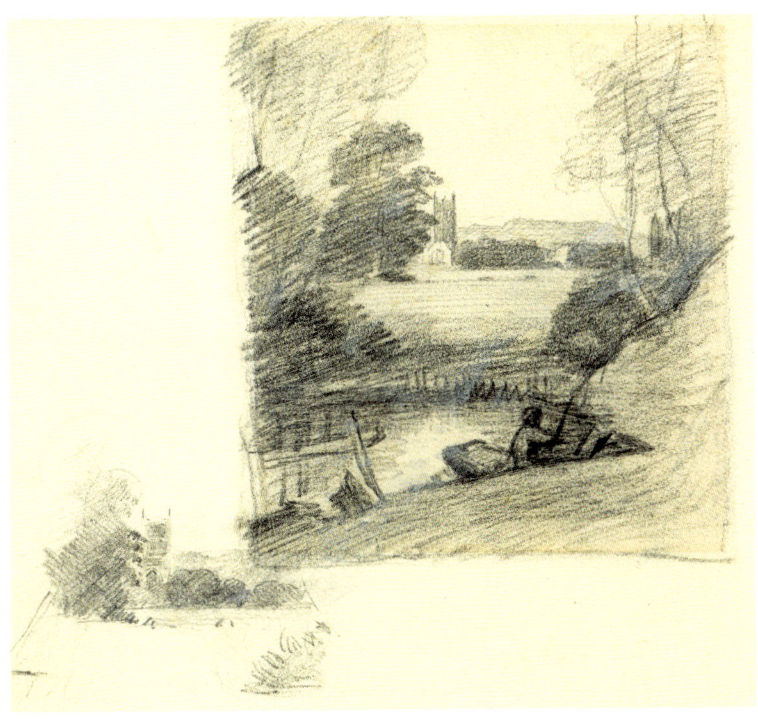

48

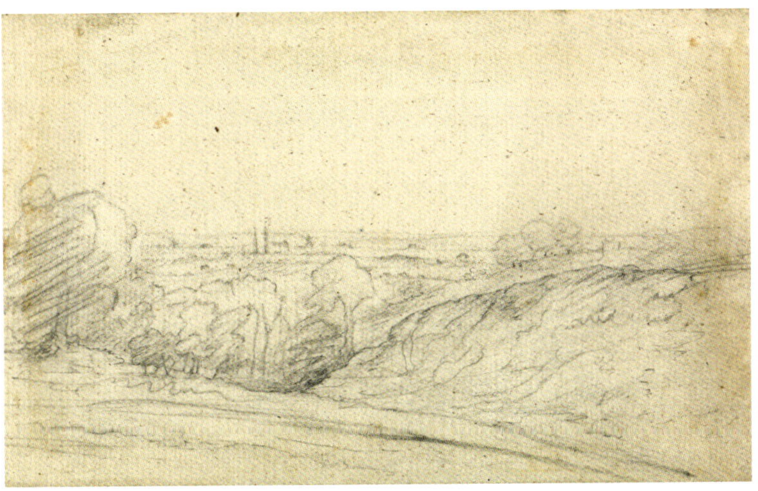

49

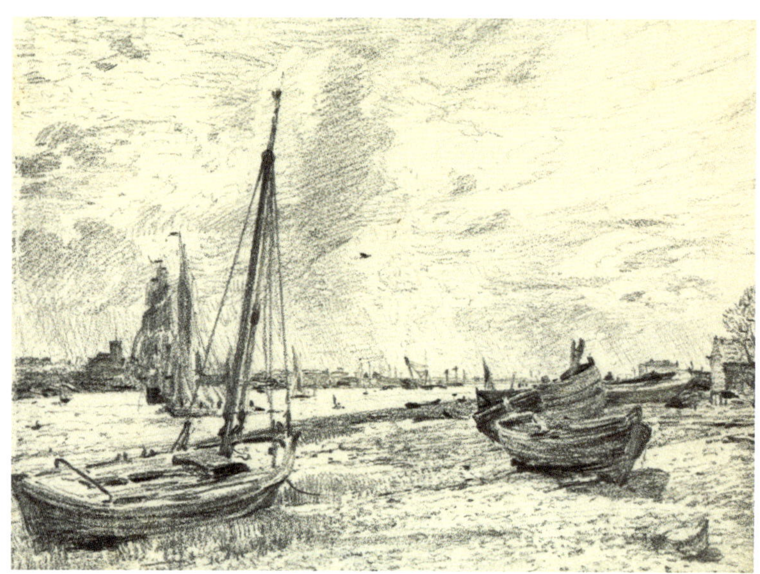
50

50
Shipping on the Thames ca. 1818
graphite, 3⅞ × 5⅛ in. (9.8 × 13 cm)

51
Fulham Church from across the River 1818
graphite, 11⅝ × 17⅜ in. (29.5 × 44.1 cm)

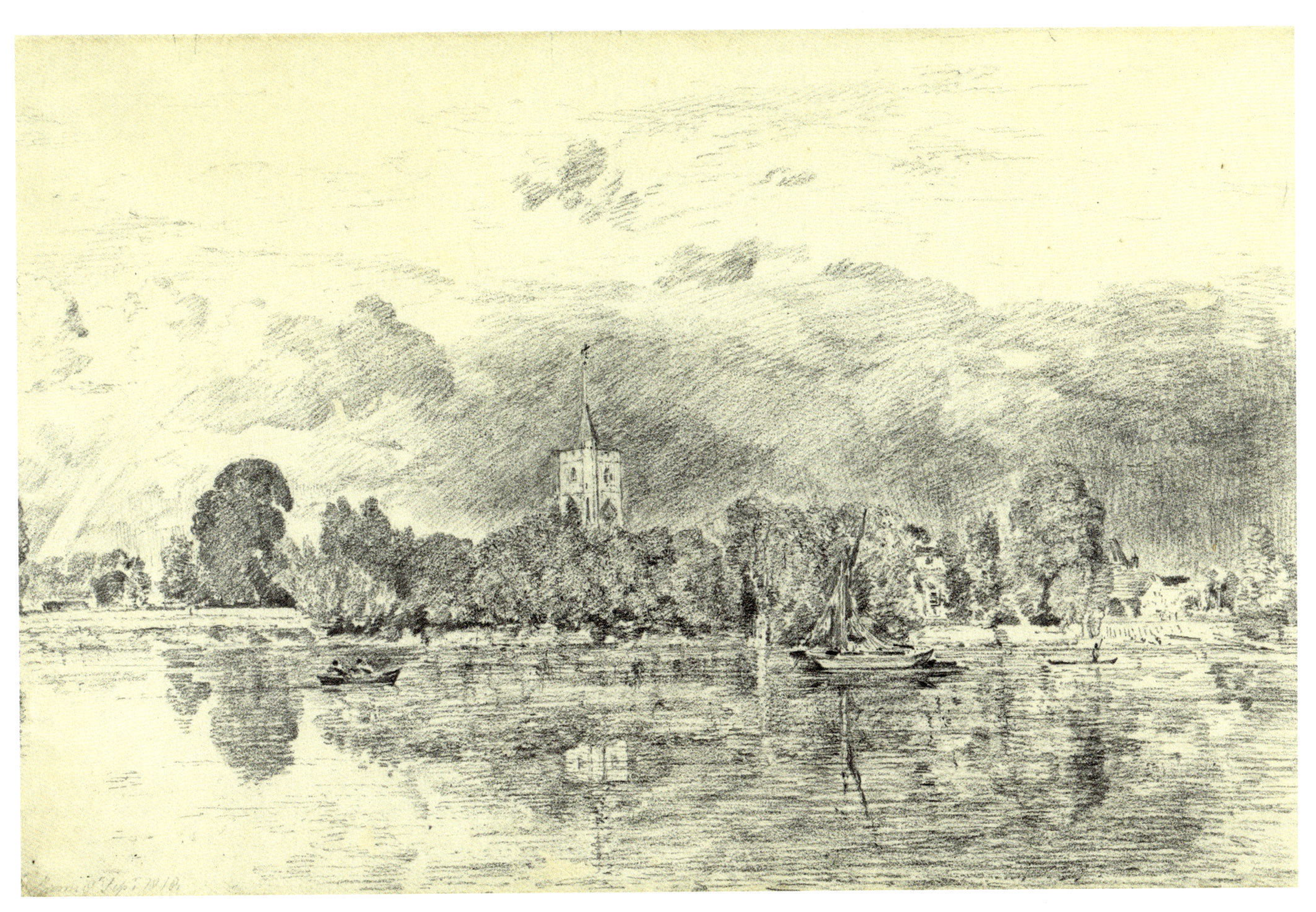

51

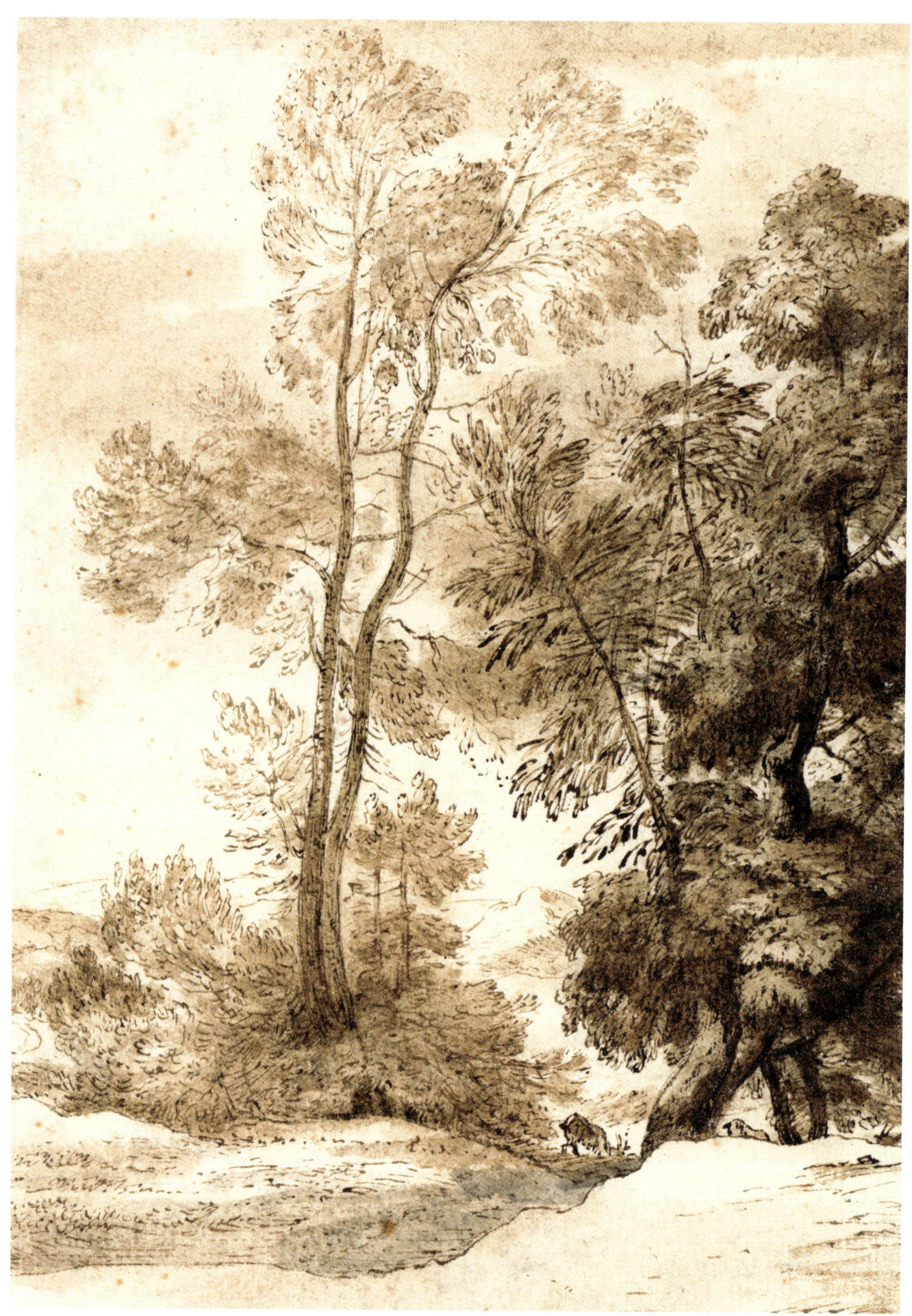

52

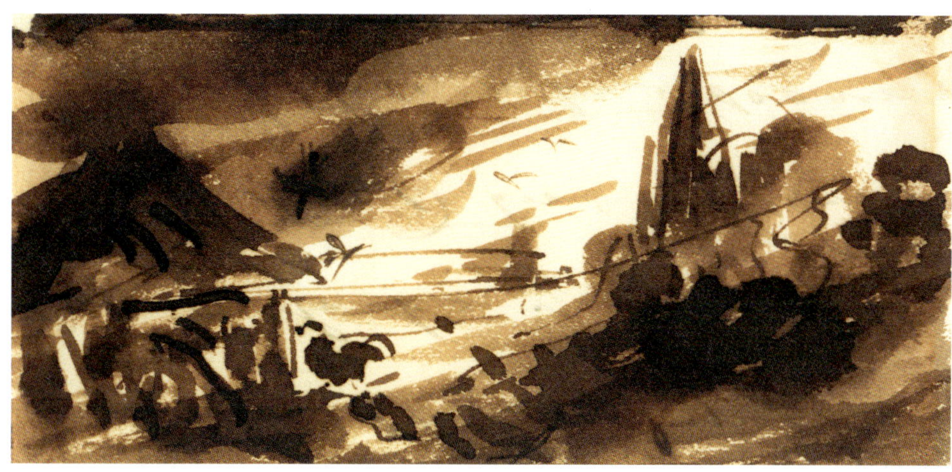
53

52
Trees and Deer 1825
pen and brown ink and brown wash, 11⅜ × 7⅞ in. (28.9 × 20 cm)

53
Dawn 1831–32
pen and brown ink and brown wash, 2¼ × 4⅜ in. (5.7 × 11.1 cm)

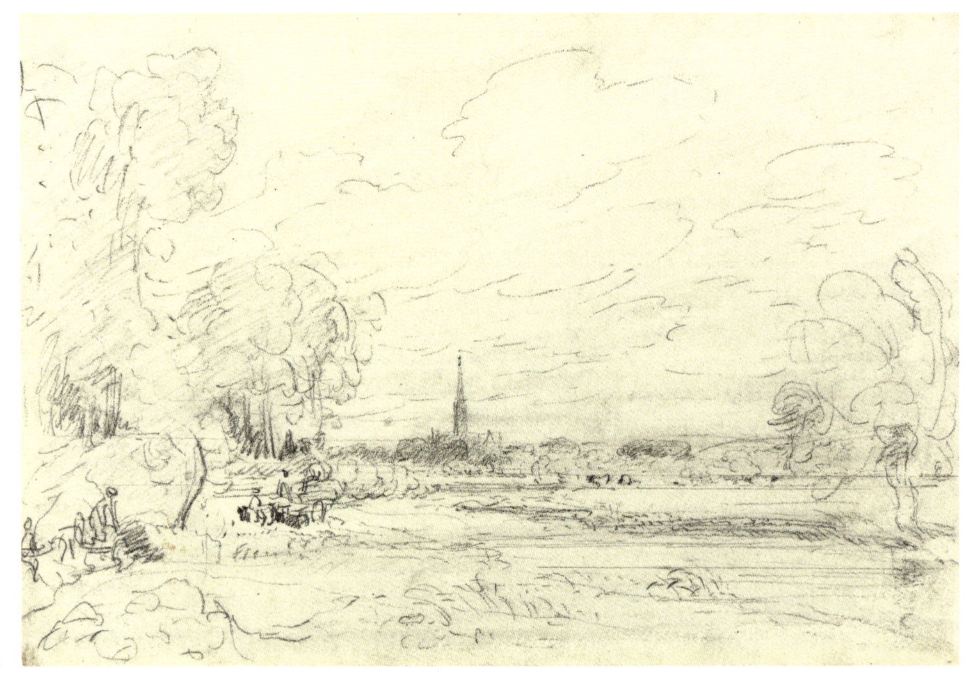

54

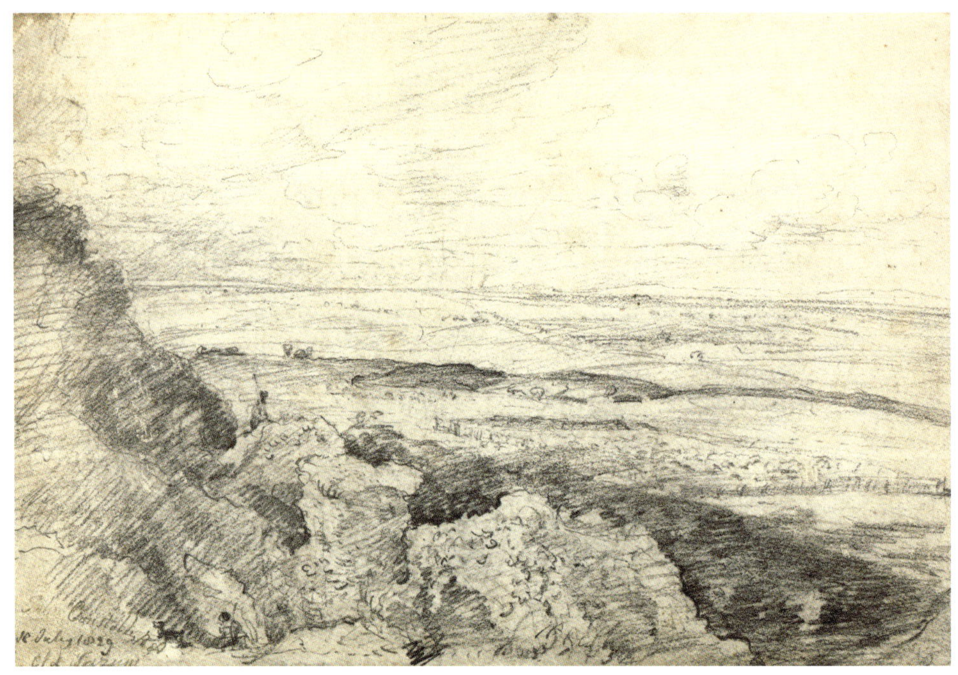

55

54
Salisbury Cathedral from the Meadows 1829
graphite, 9⅜ × 13⅜ in. (23.7 × 34 cm)

55
Salisbury Plain from Old Sarum 1829
graphite, 9⅛ × 13⅛ in. (23.2 × 33.3 cm)

56
A Bridge near Salisbury Court, Perhaps Milford Bridge ca. 1829
graphite and gray wash, 9 × 13⅛ in. (22.9 × 33.3 cm)

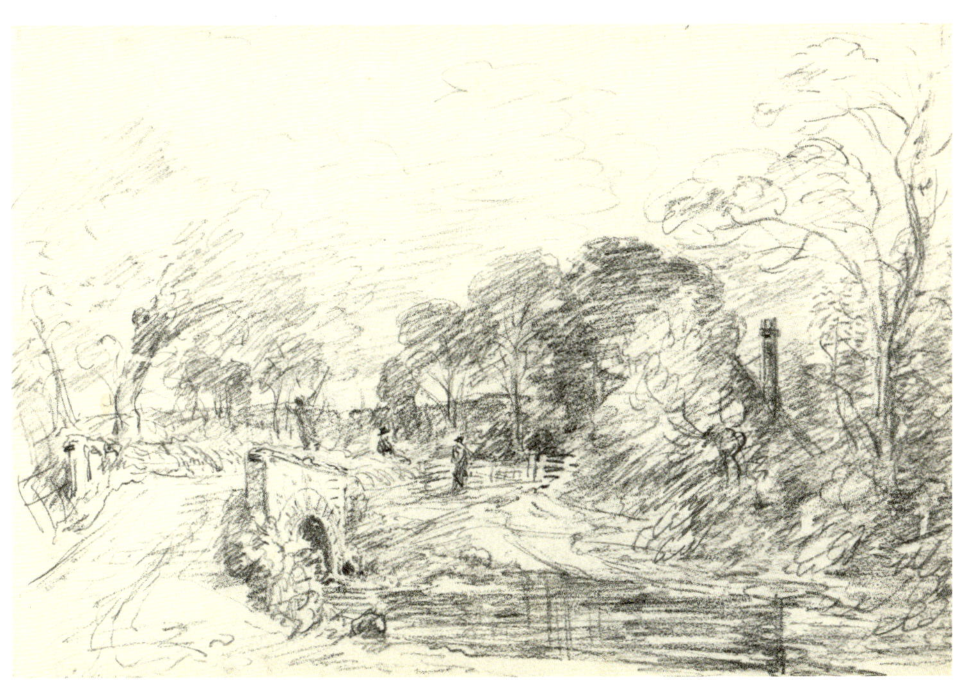

56

57 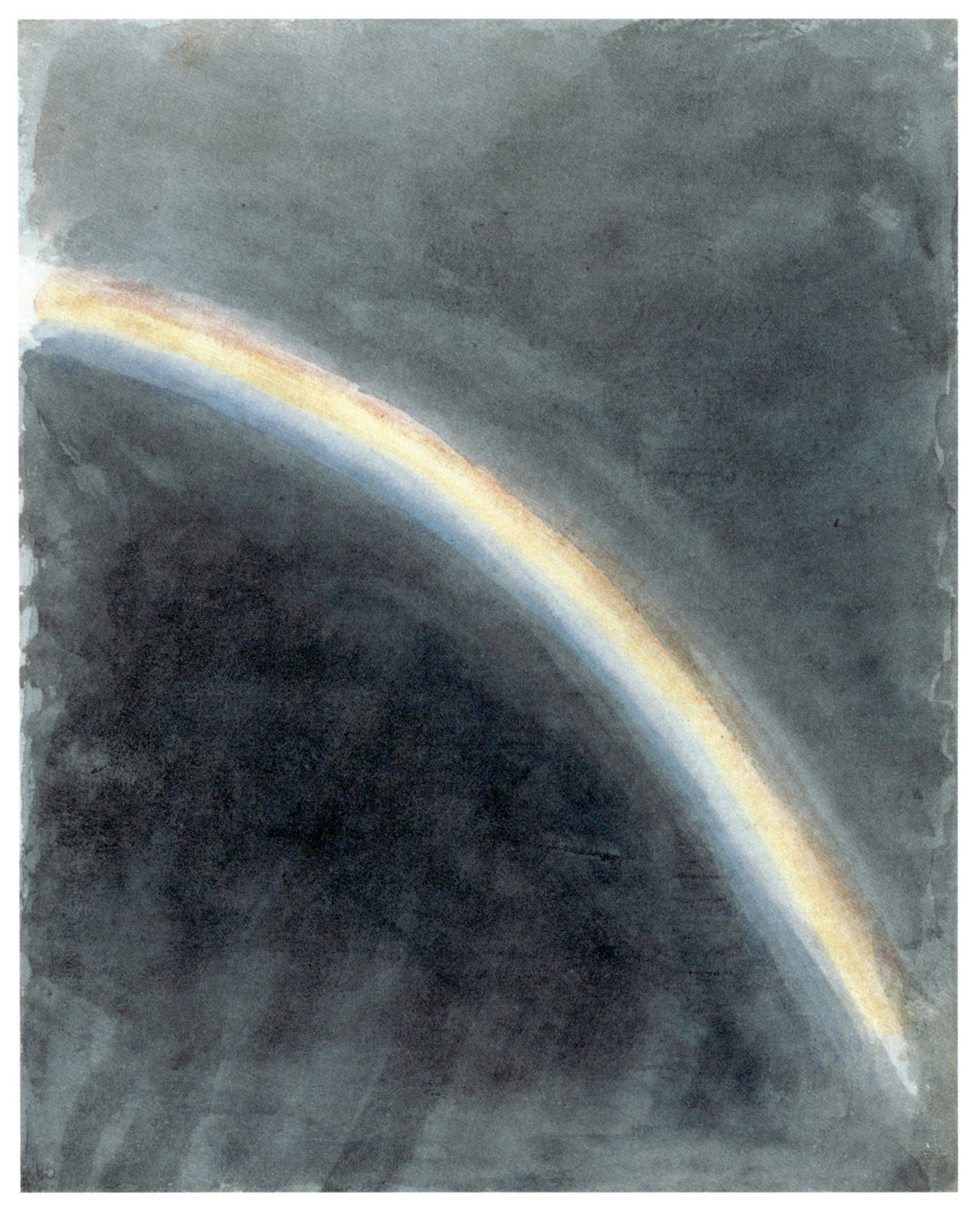

57
Sky Study with Rainbow 1827
watercolor, 8⅞ × 7¼ in. (22.5 × 18.4 cm)

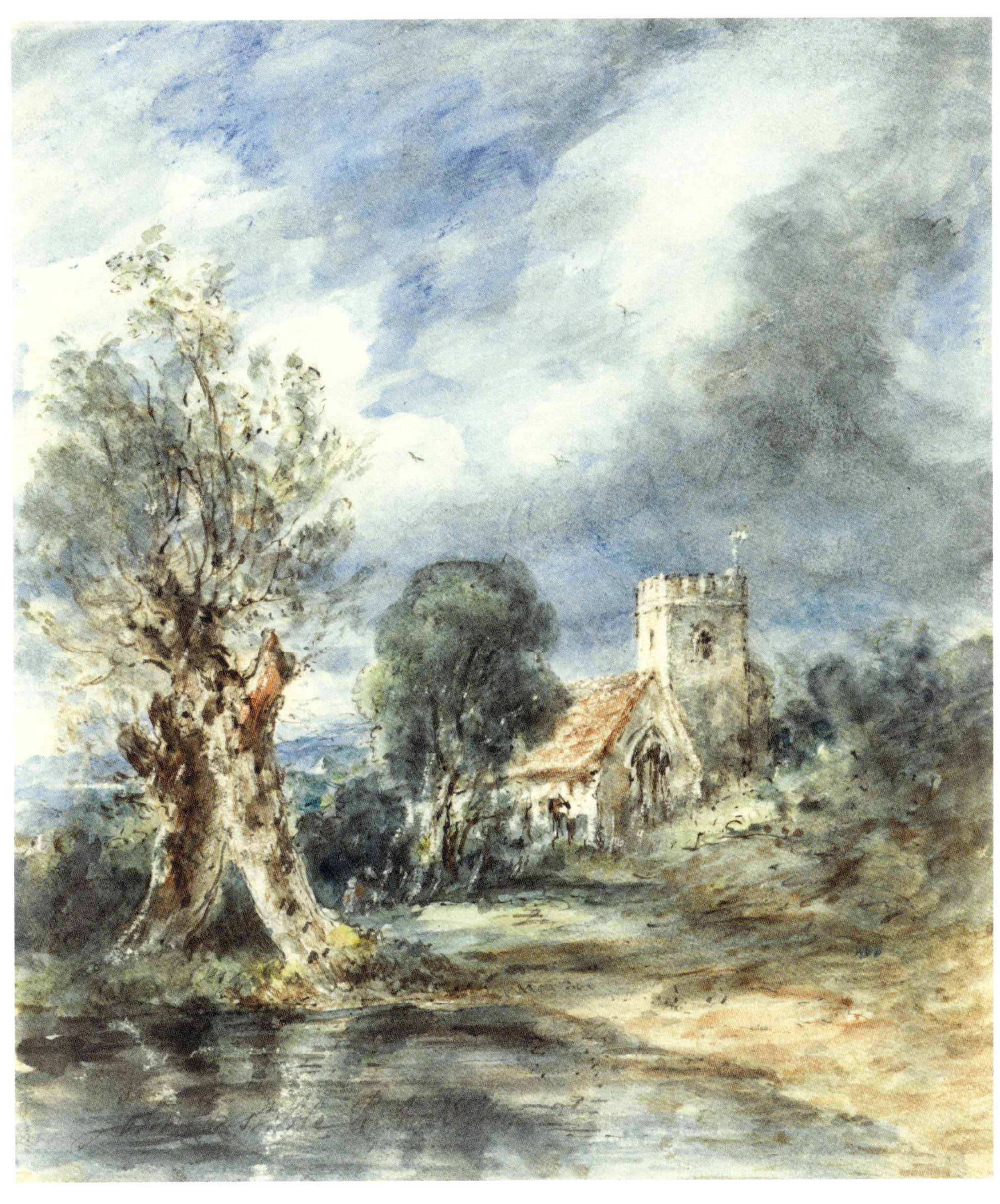

58

58
Stoke Poges Church 1834
watercolor with pen, dark brown ink,
and scratching out, 8½ × 7⅛ in. (21.6 × 18.1 cm)

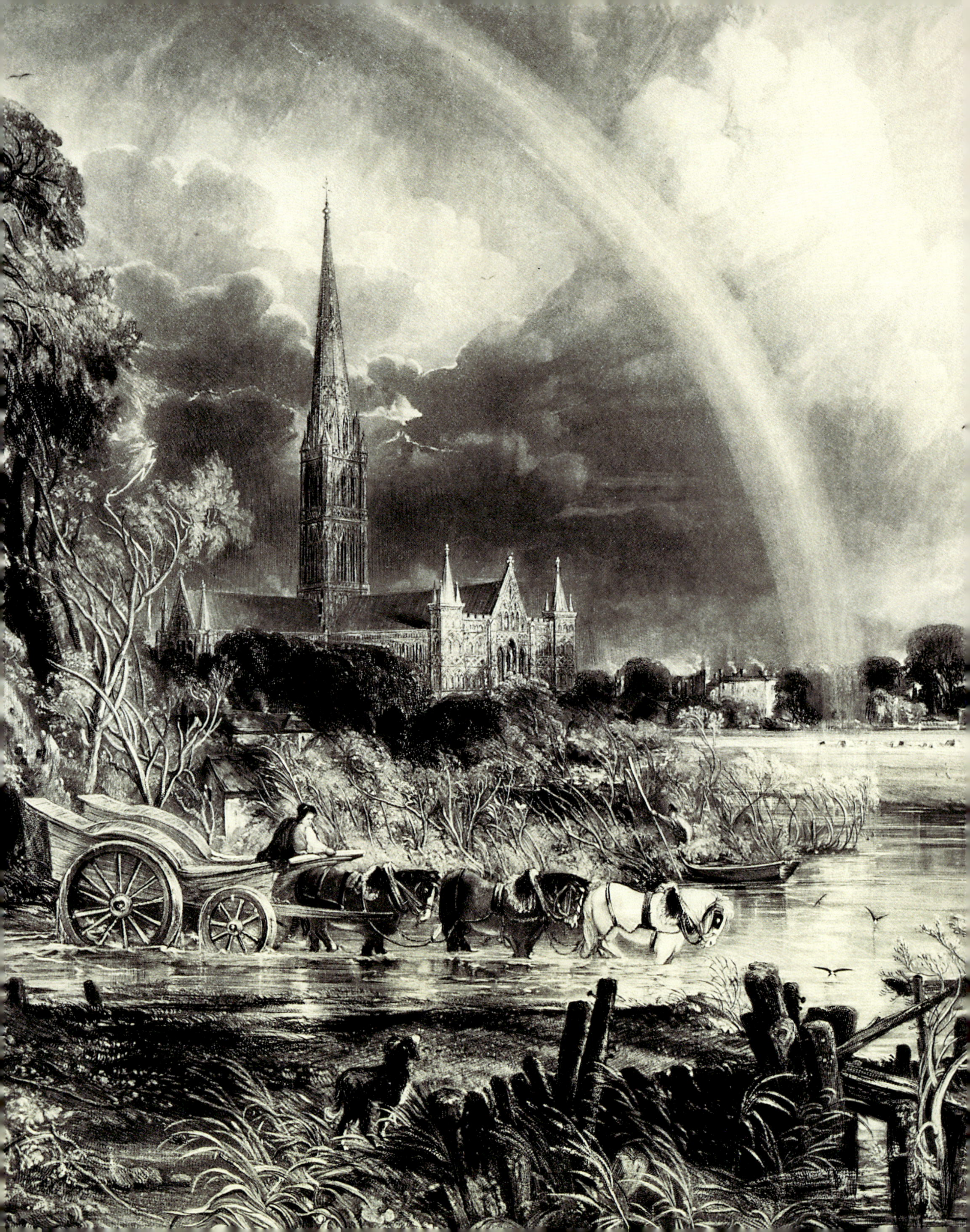

Prints

Print media dominated the visual culture of the nineteenth century. Framed, preserved in folios, bound into volumes, or even glued to walls, engravings—made on copper, steel, or wood—reached far larger audiences than oil paintings. Long apprenticeships ensured that the best engravers, whose status wavered between that of artist and artisan, attained great virtuosity, particularly in the reproduction of oil paintings.

Prints were crucial for Constable's early artistic education. In 1795 he made copies, in pen and ink, of engravings by Nicolas Dorigny (1658–1746) after the famed cartoons (designs for tapestries) by Raphael (1483–1520). The transcriptions were good enough to impress George Beaumont, and inaugurated Constable's lifelong interest in copying and collecting prints. At the time of his death, a friend recalled, the walls of the artist's bedroom "were covered with engravings." The posthumous 1838 sale of his collection included such distinguished works as Schelte Adams Bolswert's engravings after the landscapes of Rubens and nine etchings by Rembrandt.

Following the death of Maria and his belated election to full membership in the Royal Academy, Constable began to focus intensively on printmaking and publishing. Looking, perhaps, to posterity, the painter reviewed his career, selecting works that he considered to be of particular value, in terms both of artistic merit and personal association. The result was a series of twenty-two mezzotint engravings produced by the much younger Lucas, with Constable's close involvement. Issued under the cumbersome title *Various Subjects of Landscape, Characteristic of English Scenery, from Pictures Painted by John Constable, R.A.*, the work is generally known as *English Landscape*. The plan was to demonstrate to the public the variety of nature in England, its moods at different times of the day and year, captured in Constable's paintings. The undertaking was presented as an exercise in naturalism, the "just observation of natural scenery in its various aspects."

Salisbury Cathedral 1837 (detail of plate 67)

The immediate precursor to this project was Turner's celebrated *Liber Studiorum*, produced in fourteen issues between 1807 and 1819, itself titled in homage to Claude's *Liber Veritatis*, an illustrated record of the artist's compositions. Turner's magnum opus was intended both as a display of mastery across a wide range of subject matter and a theoretical treatise, though the planned explanatory letterpress was never completed. In a competitive spirit, Constable bridled against Turner's "liber stupidorum."

Mezzotint was chosen for *English Landscape* because it could find an equivalent for painterly effects: rich, velvet areas of darkness contrasted with patches of brilliant white light. Constable was unrelenting in his demands on Lucas; his letters are filled with anger and despair. Looking at a proof of *A Summerland*, he claimed that the print "is and ever will be as rotten as cow dung." Most surprising was Constable's decision to base the mezzotints not on watercolors or drawings specially prepared for translation into print, as was Turner's typical practice, but rather on existing materials, ranging from slight sketches to six-footers. *Spring* (plate 63), for example, was based on a loosely worked oil sketch (known as *Spring: East Bergholt Common*, ca. 1814, Victoria and Albert Museum) painted on a panel only 7½ inches high.

The final version of each image evolved slowly through many proof stages, during which Constable often brusquely annotated Lucas's work, or modified it with ink and even white paint in so-called touched progress proofs. In the letterpress for *Spring*, Constable commented, "This plate may perhaps give some idea of one of those bright and animated days of the early year, when all nature bears so exhilarated an aspect; when at noon large garish clouds, surcharged with hail or sleet, sweep with their broad cool shadows on the fields, woods and hills." That such effects could be conveyed so convincingly in mezzotint testifies to the success of Constable's collaboration with Lucas.

The second edition of *English Landscape* appeared in 1833 with a new subtitle, *Principally Intended to Mark the Phenomena of Chiar'Oscuro of Nature*. What had been a portfolio of cherished images was reordered to constitute an aesthetic treatise. Chiaroscuro, the contrast of light and shade in a pictorial composition, was associated with historical painters such as Caravaggio and Rembrandt; Constable, however, was interested in the effects of light and shade in nature. For him, chiaroscuro was the "medium by which the grand and varied aspects of Landscape are displayed, both in the fields and on canvass."

Lucas also prepared independent mezzotints of some of Constable's major works on much larger plates. In December 1834 the final oil version of *Salisbury Cathedral from the Meadows* (see p. 31, fig. 21) was sent to Lucas's studio. Progress was slow and there were many proof stages. After begging the engraver one last time to ensure that the rainbow was "evanescent and lovely—in the highest degree," Constable approved a final proof on March 29, 1837 (plate 67). Two days later, he died. The mezzotint, pushing its medium to the limits to match the visual and conceptual grandeur of the painting, forms a worthy epitaph to Constable's career.

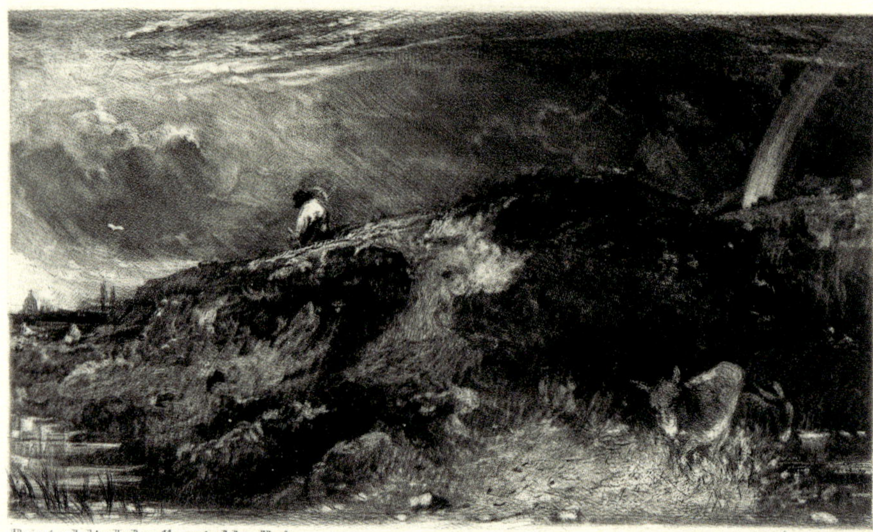

59

59
David Lucas (English, 1802–1881) after John Constable
Vignette, Hampstead Heath, Middlesex 1831
(from *English Landscape*) mezzotint, 11¾ × 17⅜ in. (29.8 × 44.1 cm)

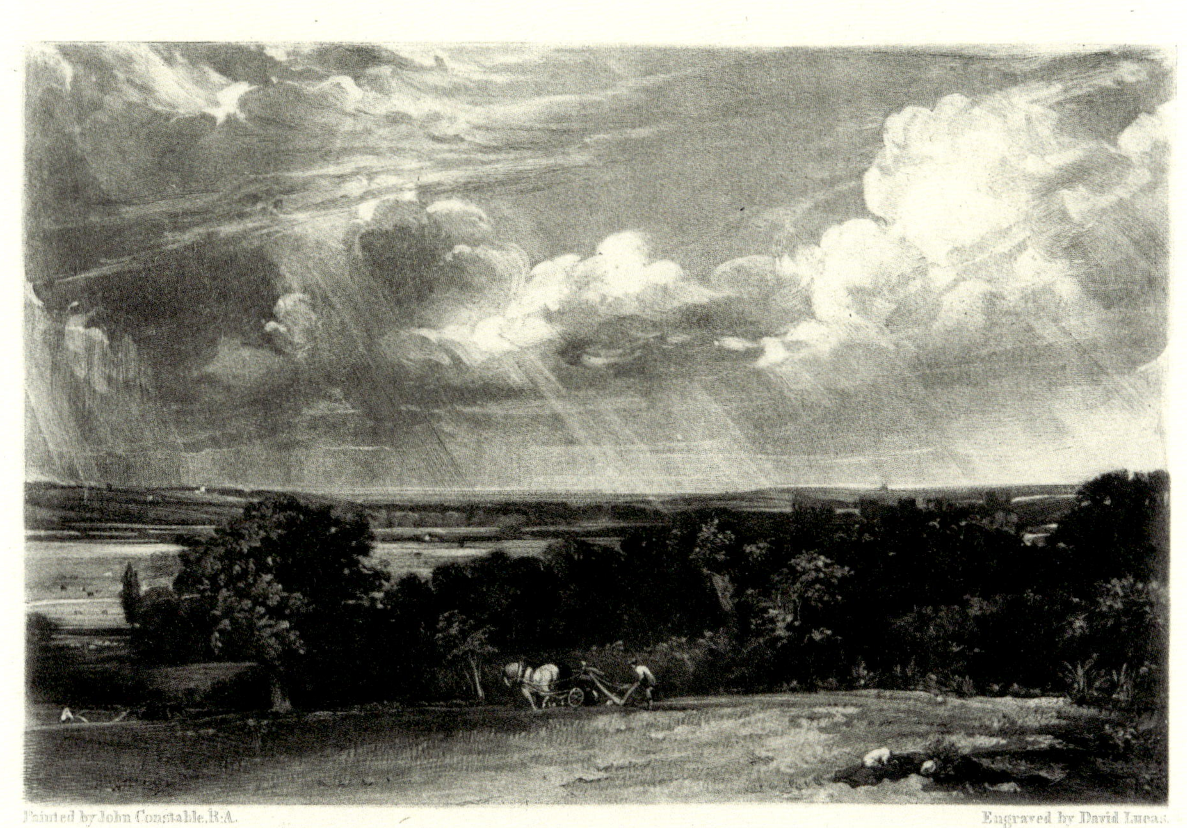

60

60
David Lucas after John Constable
A Summerland 1831
(from *English Landscape*) mezzotint and drypoint,
12 × 17¼ in. (30.5 × 43.8 cm)
GIFT OF MRS. JOHN ARCHER GEE FOR HISTORY OF ART (HISTORY OF PRINTS), TRANSFERRED FROM YALE UNIVERSITY ART GALLERY

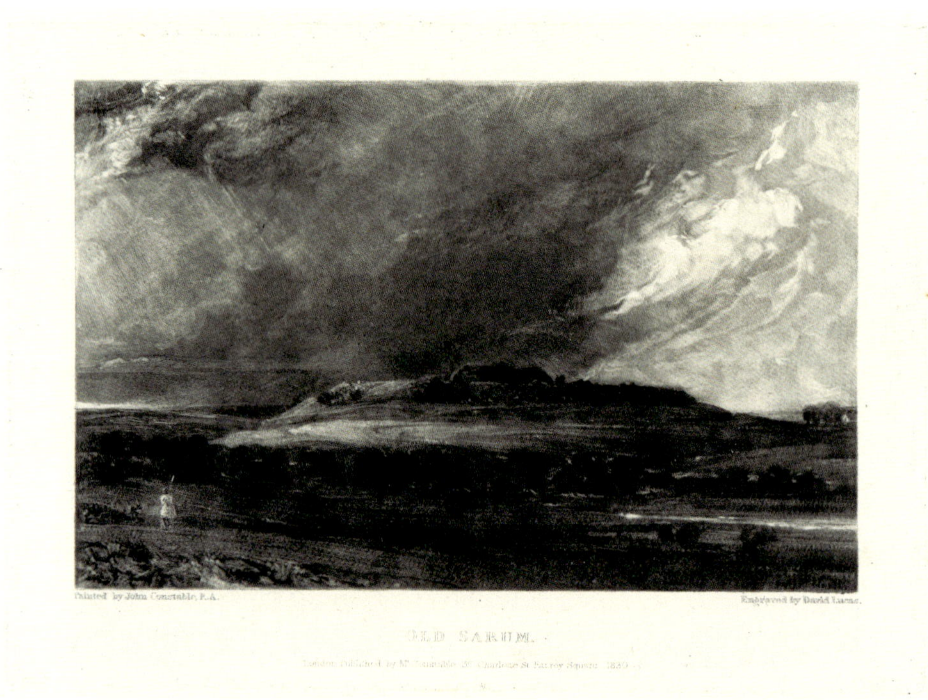
61

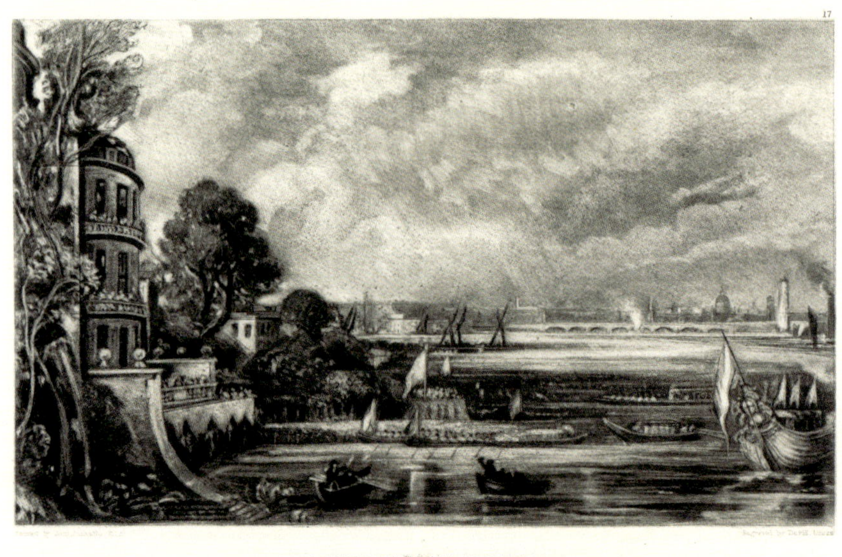
62

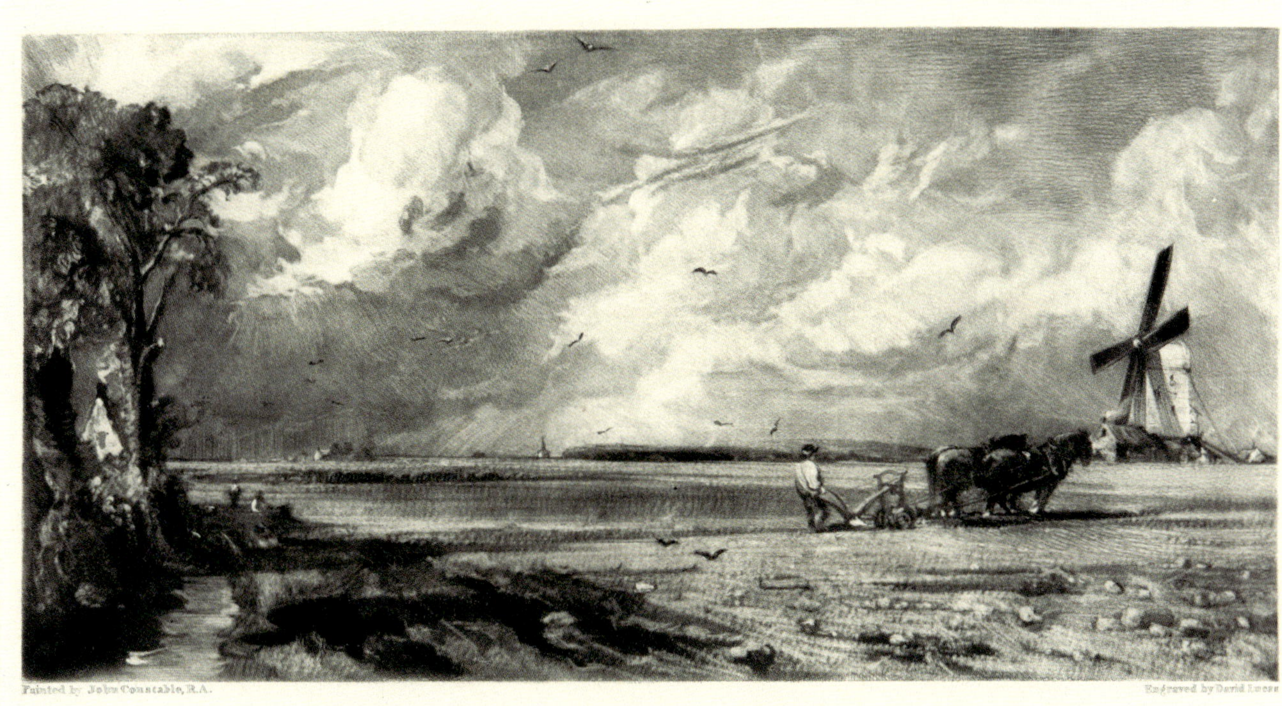

63

61
David Lucas after John Constable
Old Sarum 1829–30
(from *English Landscape*) mezzotint, 7⅛ × 9⅞ in.
(18.1 × 25.1 cm)

62
David Lucas after John Constable
Opening of Waterloo Bridge 1831
(from *English Landscape*) mezzotint and drypoint,
9 × 11¾ in. (22.9 × 29.8 cm)

63
David Lucas after John Constable
Spring 1829–30
(from *English Landscape*) mezzotint and drypoint,
11⅝ × 17¼ in. (29.5 × 43.8 cm)
TRANSFERRED FROM YALE UNIVERSITY ART GALLERY

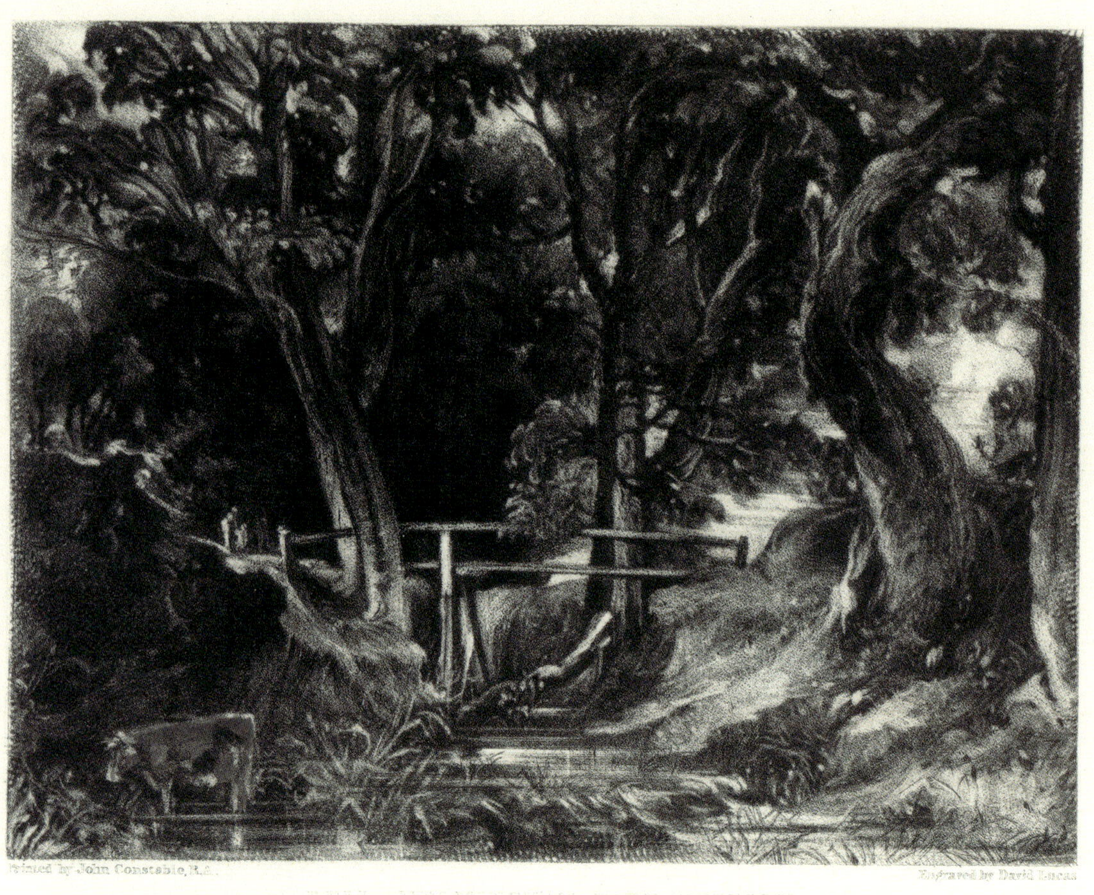

64

64
David Lucas after John Constable
A Dell, Helmingham Park, Suffolk 1830
(from *English Landscape*) mezzotint and drypoint with graphite, 11¾ × 17½ in. (29.8 × 44.5 cm)
GIFT OF MRS. JOHN ARCHER GEE FOR HISTORY OF ART (HISTORY OF PRINTS), TRANSFERRED FROM YALE UNIVERSITY ART GALLERY

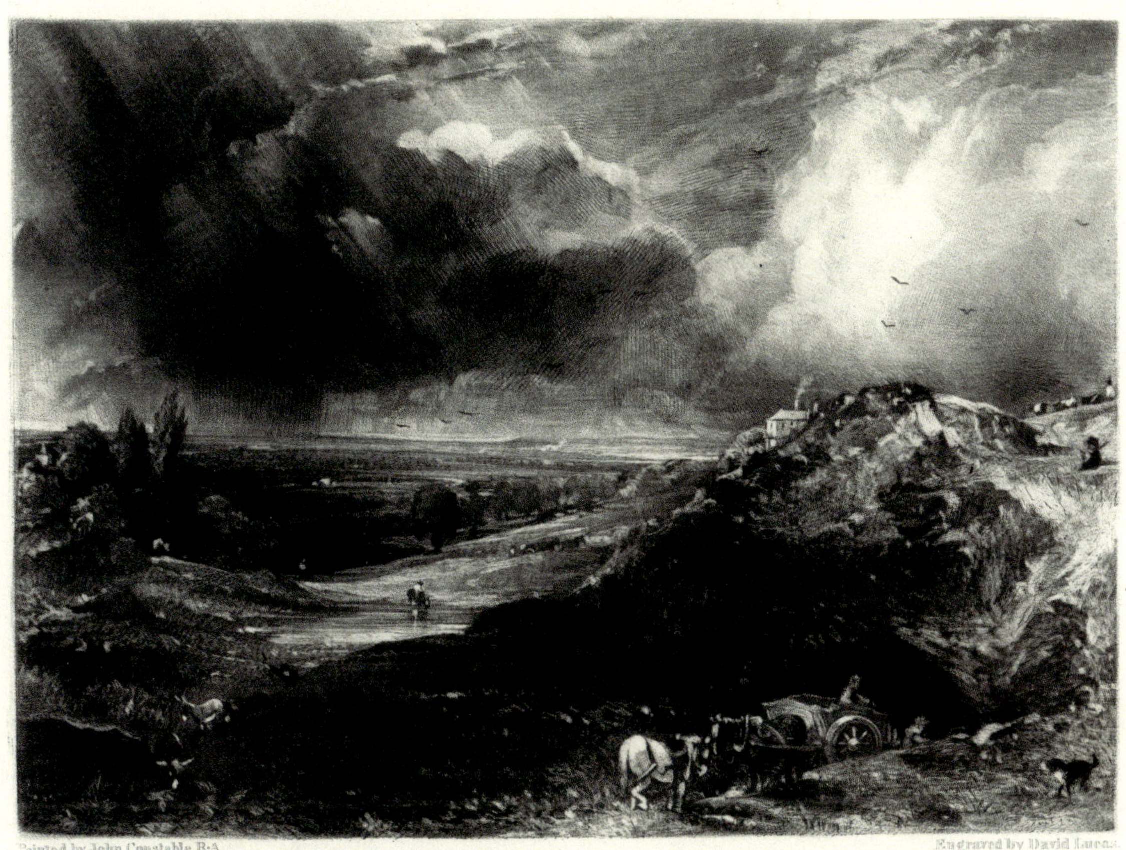

65

65
David Lucas after John Constable
A Heath 1831
(from *English Landscape*) mezzotint, 11¾ × 17¼ in. (29.8 × 43.8cm)
TRANSFERRED FROM YALE UNIVERSITY ART GALLERY

66
David Lucas after John Constable
Hadleigh Castle, Large Plate 1830–32
mezzotint and etching, 13 × 18 in. (33 × 45.7 cm)

67
David Lucas after John Constable
Salisbury Cathedral 1837
mezzotint and etching, 26¾ × 31½ in. (67.9 × 80 cm)

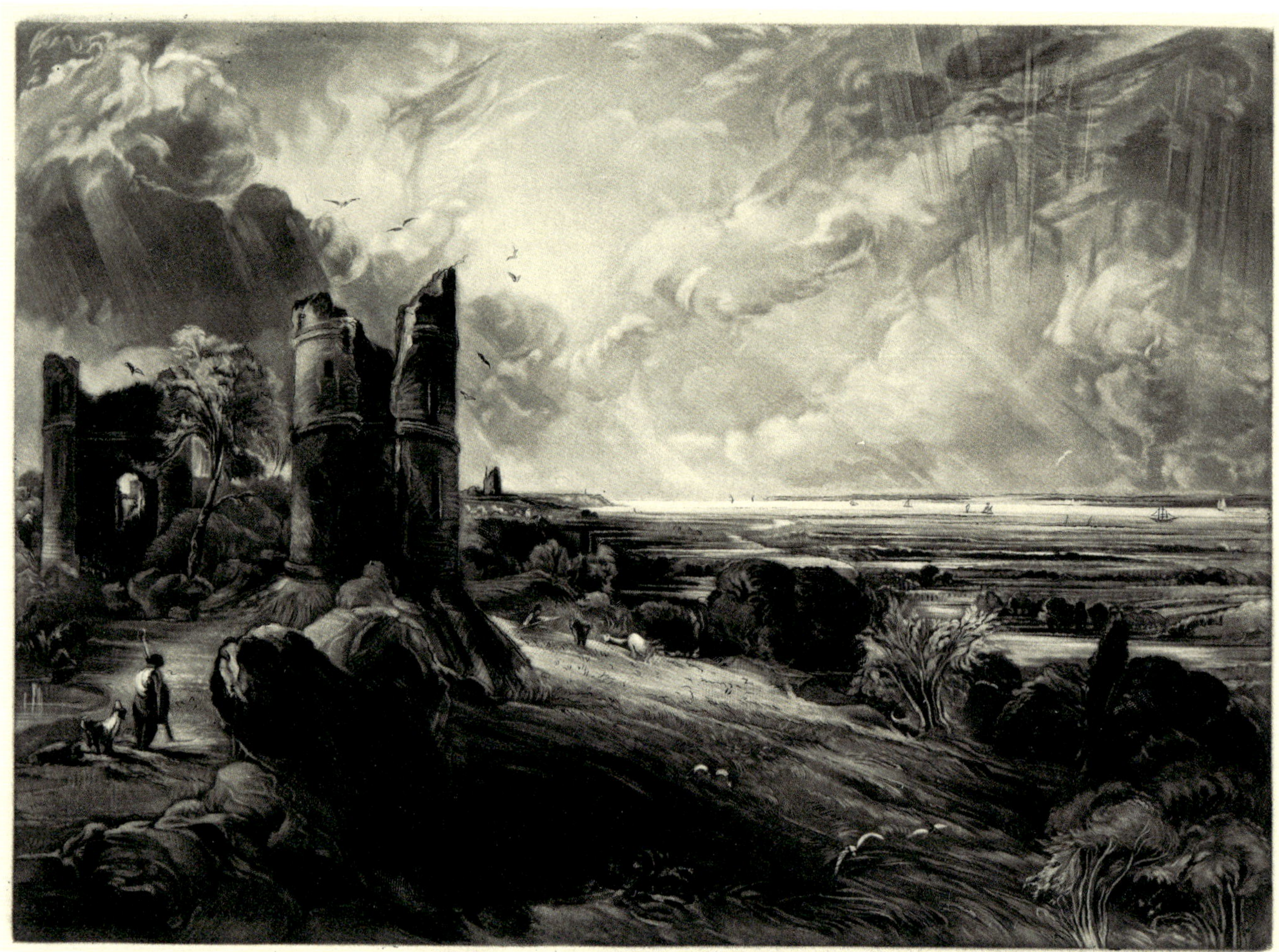

66

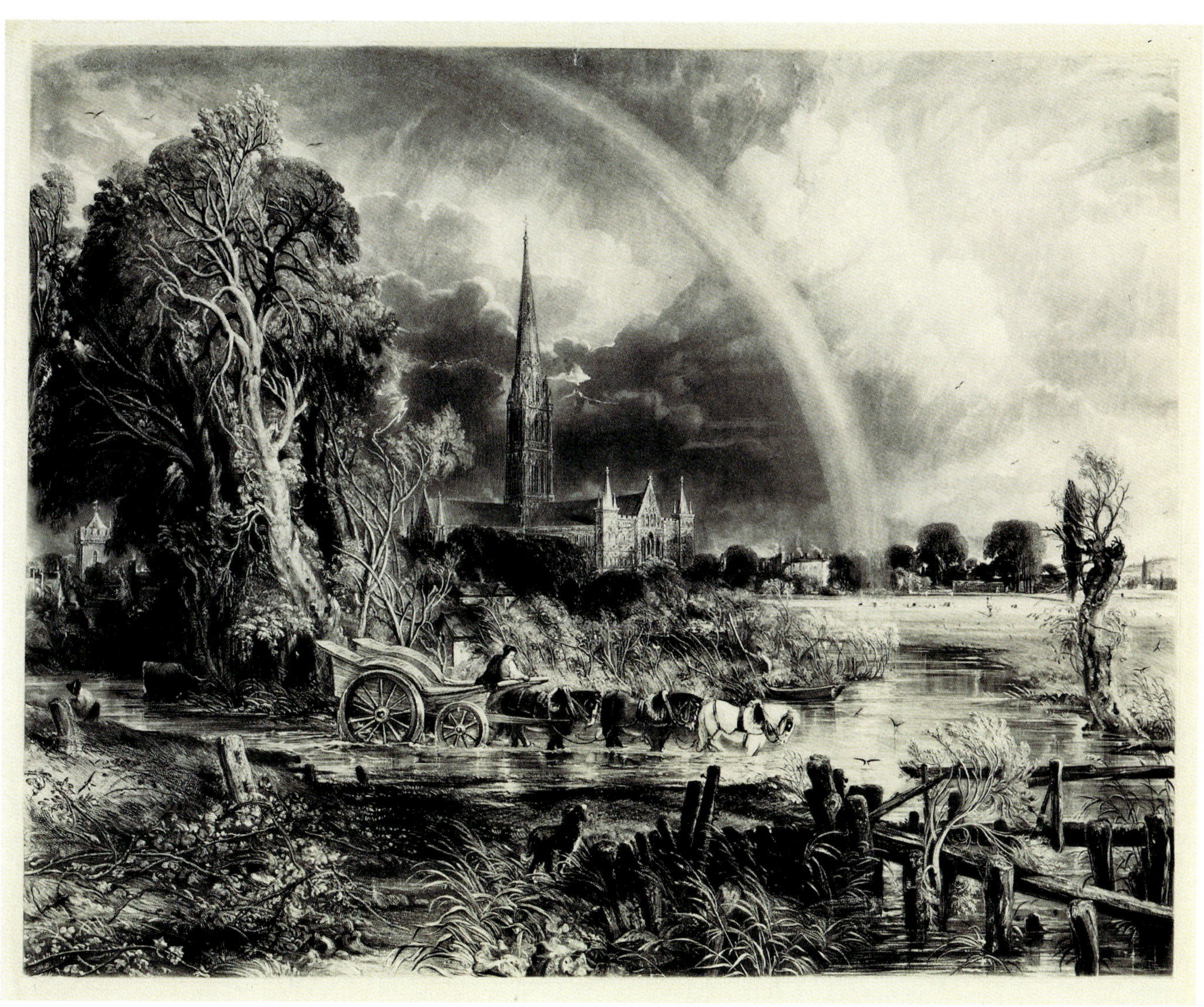

67

"Little, Nameless, Unremembered": Constable's Clouds

Nicholas Robbins

In May 1838, a year after John Constable's death, the paintings remaining in his studio were sold by auction at Messrs. Foster and Son on Pall Mall in London. Alongside paintings of "grand subjects" (as the auction catalogue described them) attendees of this sale would have seen a group of twenty-nine of Constable's oil sketches of "Clouds and Skies." Unless they had visited the artist's studio during his lifetime, it was unlikely they would have encountered these works before. These small studies, capturing the movement of vapor and the play of color and light, are now some of the best-known works by the artist. The largest number of them were made between 1820 and 1823 on Hampstead Heath, an open commons on the outskirts of London where, beginning in 1819, Constable lived for part of the year, mainly during the summer or autumn months. The cloud studies represent much of what we value in the artist's work: intimacy with nature's vitality, close attention to the familiar and the everyday, and experimentation with the materiality of paint. These slight oil sketches, in fact, might stand in for Romanticism itself. They mark a moment when artists wanted to turn away from classical models and academic strictures to discover new forms and new feelings: to find, in William Wordsworth's words, "A motion and a spirit, that impels / All thinking things, all objects of thought, / and rolls through all things." Constable's cloud studies were investigations of transient configurations of suspended water shot through by light. But they were also attempts to understand the physical and

Cloud Study 1822 (detail of plate 27)

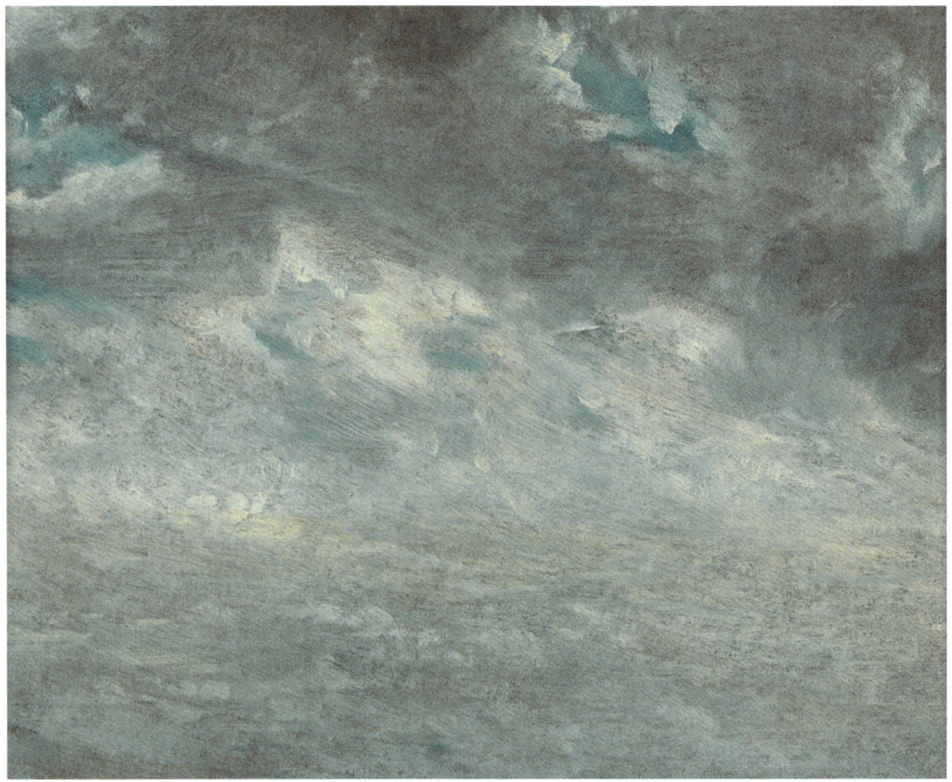

FIG. 1 John Constable, *Cloud Study*, 1821, oil on paper, mounted on board, 9¾ × 11⅞ in. (24.8 × 30.2 cm). Except where otherwise noted, all figures Yale Center for British Art, Paul Mellon Collection

psychological structure of experience itself—to find, in these momentary shapes, a way to "see into the life of things."

Reporting on the sale of Constable's effects, a writer in the cultural journal *The Athenaeum* admitted that "to some . . . his scenes show too much of our moist climate." An oil sketch painted on September 13, 1821, one of dozens of similar studies that Constable made in these years, might be a good example (fig. 1). The image is almost entirely composed of white and gray clouds. We can follow the marks of Constable's brush in the furrows of paint: long gestures dragging scumbled pigment over the surface; fields of thicker, curving marks that capture denser vapor; energetic passages that suggest movement and animation. In the darker field at the top of the image, light has been blocked by the clouds. While the image is flat, the phenomena it records are not. Constable manages to capture something of the straining arch of the sky as it passes from the distant atmosphere at the bottom of the image toward the upper register, which is, in effect, above him. The edge of the picture is arbitrary. It is a fragment snatched from a wider continuum, which nevertheless captures a sense of movement across and beyond this frame. This sense is echoed by the inscription that Constable added, as he did with most of his cloud studies, to the back of the image: "Sept'r 13th one o'clock. Slight wind at North West, which became tempestuous in the afternoon, with rain all the night following." We are placed in a moment and a time of day—"one o'clock"—and given access to sensations not captured in the image (like the wind that gently blows). The inscription also records what came after this image: the "tempestuous" weather and rain that were heralded by the momentary forms captured in the study. We see this image as a study of not just shape, color, and light but also natural history (as science was then called). The shapes of the clouds are connected to a continuum of time and experience. They unlock a wider field of knowledge.

Sketching outdoors required artists to fundamentally reimagine the practices of art, both philosophical and material. Painting was, in the academic tradition, an activity that took place indoors, in the studio. This sequestering of painting away from the world was part of what allowed artists to claim their work as an intellectual and genteel pursuit, rather than as manual labor. To paint outside, as Constable had since the early years of his career, he needed to move into the changeable air of the world beyond the studio, like the figure he sketched sitting on Hampstead Heath in September 1820 (fig. 2). In some ways, this practice

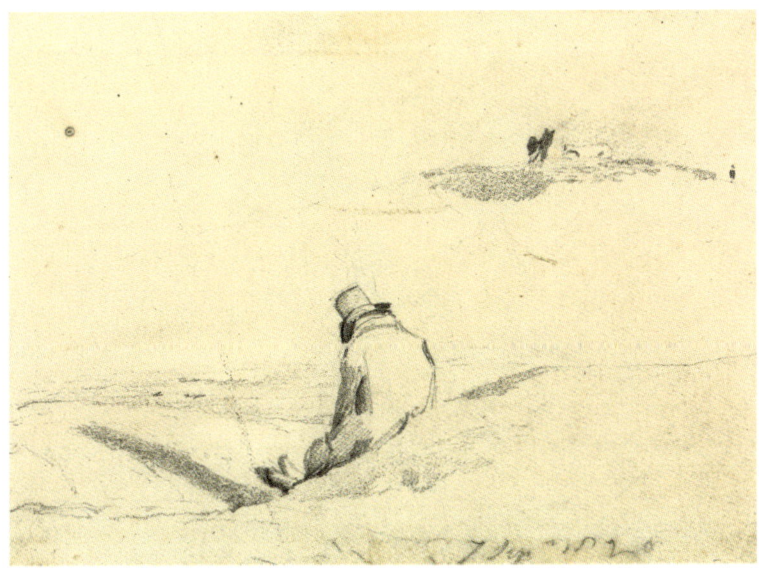

FIG. 2 John Constable, *Hampstead Heath*, 1820, graphite, 3¼ × 4⅞ in. (8.3 × 12.4 cm)

brought him closer to the conditions of the agricultural work that furnished the subject for so much of his art, though he would almost always view it from the distance of the landowner. But it also chimed with an increasing emphasis in natural history on the importance of observation and knowledge gained "in the field"—where immersion in the perpetually moving matter of the environment demanded its own kind of intellectual work. It was perhaps this sense of exposure to the larger forces coursing through the world, the "motion and . . . spirit" that "rolls through all things," that kept Constable's attention so closely focused on the clouds. Here, what the artist called the "chiaro'scuro of nature"—the flickering relations between light and dark that he saw as the key formal patterning of the world—found free play in a visual field reduced to fine gradations of light and shadow. That is to say, the cloud studies are as much a mode of experimenting with image-making as they are a mode of producing knowledge.

This dedication to plein air painting was not unprecedented. One of the artist's key models, the seventeenth-century painter Claude Lorrain, was said to have sketched out of doors in Rome. (As Constable put it, Claude "lived in the fields all day, and drew at the Academy at night.") Plein air sketching was practiced by the prominent French academician Pierre-Henri de Valenciennes and promoted by him in his *Elémens de perspective pratique* (1799), one of the most important books on landscape painting in Constable's time. British landscape painters before him, like Thomas Jones, had produced striking oil sketches (fig. 3). Likewise, the classificatory impulse that guided natural-historical study

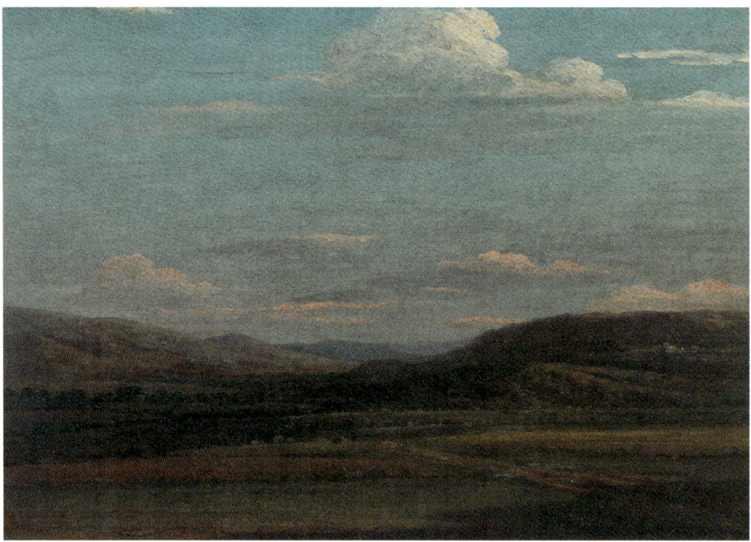

FIG. 3 Thomas Jones (English, 1742–1803), *The Vale of Pencerrig*, 1776, oil on paper, 9¼ × 12¾ in. (23.5 × 32.4 cm)

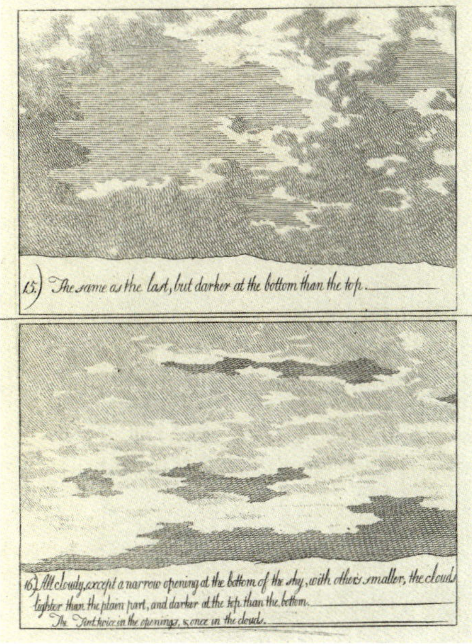

FIG. 4 Alexander Cozens (English, 1717–1786), illustrations of cloud forms (from *A New Method of Assisting the Invention in Drawing Original Compositions of Landscape* [1785]), etching, 4⅜ × 1⅛ in. (11 × 15.5 cm). Yale University, Beinecke Rare Book and Manuscript Library

also took shape in artistic practice. Alexander Cozens's *A New Method of Assisting the Invention in Drawing Original Compositions of Landscape* (1785) included a catalogue of skies that painters might use to populate their landscapes (fig. 4). Constable would copy these etchings in small graphite sketches, now in the Courtauld Gallery, sometime in the early 1820s. He was also far from alone in his deep interest in studying the sky. Many fellow artists, such as John Linnell (fig. 5), studied the shifting effects of light and air, especially in the luminous medium of watercolor. J.M.W. Turner's watercolors, and in particular his small, handheld sketchbooks, exploit the liquidity and quickness of the medium, capturing, for example, the uncertain materiality of oceanic vapor and its thick, color-charged air (fig. 6).

Yet Constable's oil sketches remain unique in nineteenth-century European painting for their sustained exploration of a single motif—clouds and skies—and for their formal and material experimentation. Taken together, they might be understood to form a "natural history . . . of the skies," to borrow the artist's words. We find in these studies a sense of the world's unrepeatable variety: the silvery light filtering through a layer of cloud thick with moisture (plate 25); a slash of rain or wind that passes through an animated sky, achieved by a bold stroke of the brush (p. 35, fig. 24); the chance visual echo that emerges between a cloud and a tuft of foliage (fig. 7). Although the studies filtered into the ambitious "six-footer"

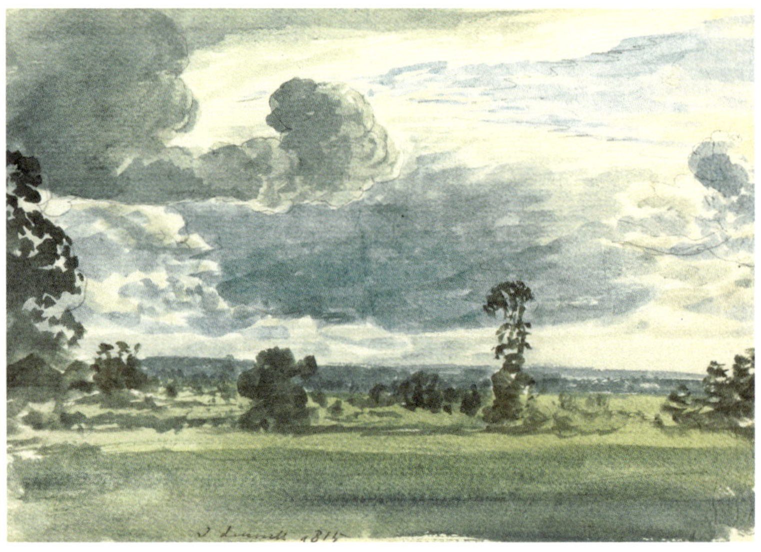

FIG. 5 John Linnell (English, 1792–1882), *A Windy Day*, 1815, watercolor over graphite, 6⅛ × 9 in. (15.6 × 22.9 cm)

FIG. 6 J. M. W. Turner (English, 1775–1851), *The Channel Sketchbook* (fol. 43v–44r), ca. 1845, sketchbook bound in red calf with marbled endpapers, 88 leaves with 74 watercolors and 26 graphite sketches, each sheet 3¾ × 6¼ in. (9.5 × 15.9 cm)

exhibition paintings that Constable was making in the 1820s, there is no direct line, no immediate transposition, from study to finished painting. The sketches seem to have been made partly for their own purpose, for the knowledge gained in the process of looking and of manipulating paint—a kind of real-time material translation of Constable's observations. As the artist's contemporary William Hazlitt wrote about painting in 1820, with "every stroke of the brush, a new field of inquiry is laid open."

FIG. 7 John Constable, *Cloud Study with Trees*, 1821, oil on paper on board, 6¾ × 12 in. (17.1 × 30.5 cm)

This experiment in depiction required experimentation with materials. In Constable's time there were likely some prepared papers available, though specialist materials for oil sketching would become more widespread among manufacturers' offerings later in the century. Constable used a variety of paper grounds for his oil sketches in the 1820s, but all of them were aimed at producing a quick-drying and easily transportable surface. Throughout his oil sketching practice, he experimented with laminating different paper grounds together, often preparing these sheets himself by laying on a painting ground and dividing the sheet into smaller, standard-size papers that he carried in his traveling paint box, with the lid serving as an easel. Constable mixed his paints using pre-ground pigments from color suppliers and kept them in small bladders (necessary before the invention of metal paint tubes in the mid-nineteenth century) that could be transported in his box-easel.

We could see Constable's experiments with painting materials as a way to secure the "freshness" of his oil sketches, not unlike the way naturalists developed methods to gather and store specimens of plants and animals collected in the field. To be "fresh" was perhaps the highest aim of Constable's art. He wanted his work to body forth, as he put it in a letter, "my 'dews'—my 'breezes'—my bloom and freshness." Freshness had to do with an idea of renovated life and renewed vitality, of painting that remained close to the shifting quality of the natural world rather than imitating the departed forms of older art. The movements

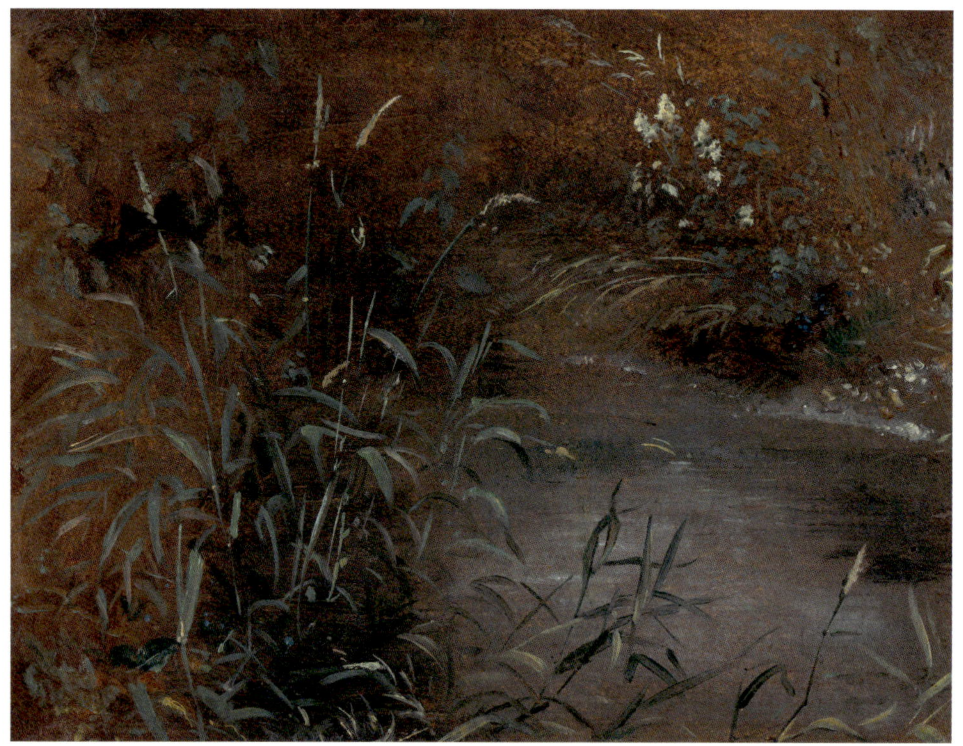

FIG. 8 John Constable, *Rushes by a Pool*, ca. 1821, oil on paper, mounted on board, 9 × 11¾ in. (22.9 × 29.8 cm)

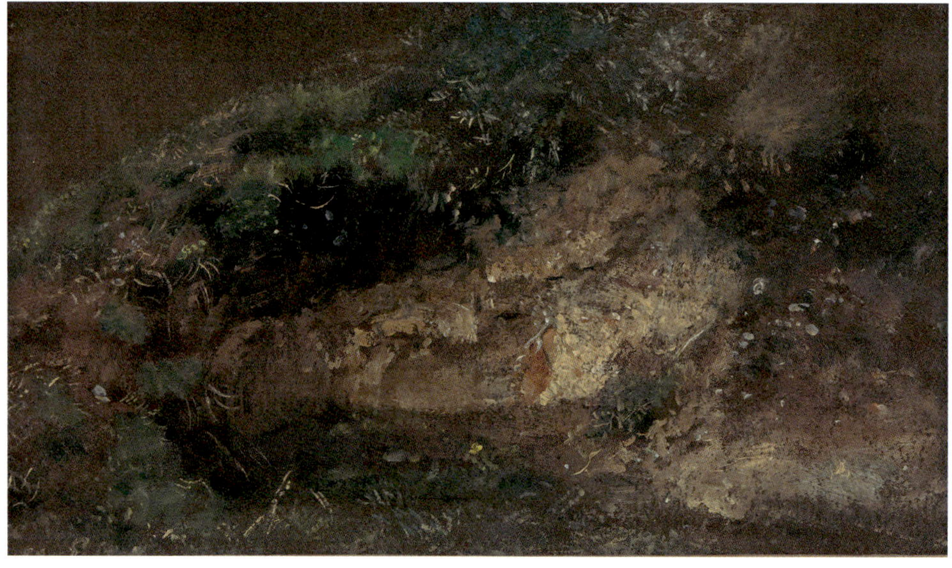

FIG. 9 John Constable, *Undergrowth*, ca. 1815, oil on paper, mounted on board, 6½ × 11½ in. (16.5 × 29.2 cm)

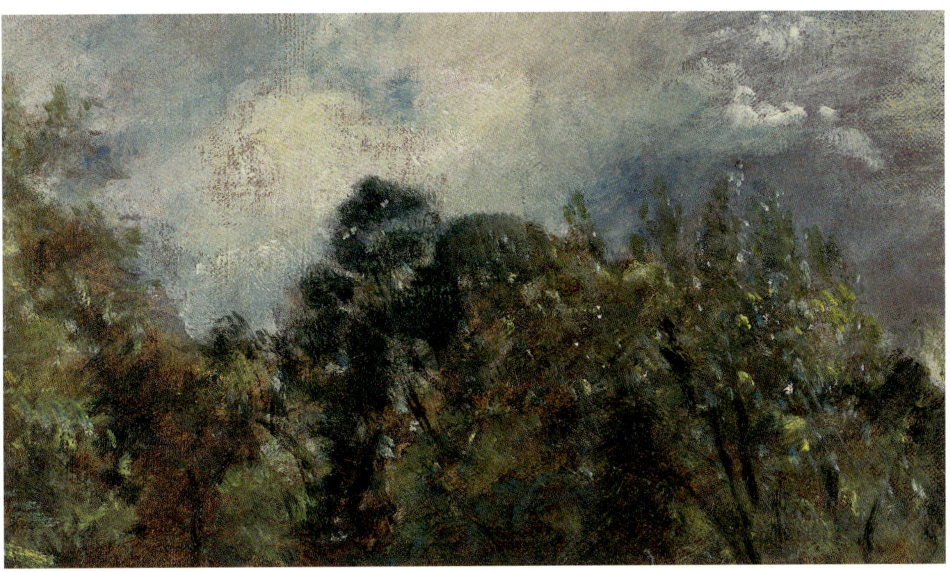

FIG. 10 John Constable, *Hampstead Heath*, ca. 1820–30 (detail of plate 24)

of air and moisture through the sky refreshed the landscape below them. The meteorologist John E. Thornes, after studying the inscriptions on the backs of the sketches, noted that Constable "liked to paint after rain, when the grass is moist and green and the leaves are glistening." And so we can put Constable's cloud studies together with his remarkable studies of plant life growing at the edge of a pool (fig. 8) or nestling into a sandy bank (fig. 9). In a small painting made in Hampstead (plate 24), the two—sky and ground—come together. The broken forms of the clouds echo the rugged, clayey soil; bright white wisps of vapor find their tonal complement in the shining of green grass. On the leaves of the tree on the right, bits of white paint evoke glistening moisture (fig. 10). The sky imparts something of its transience to the more stable elements of landscape below, interweaving the two registers of the image. This transference of freshness is captured by the material procedures of painting and the pigments that blend together in their liquid state.

In a now famous letter on the subject, written in 1821, Constable reflected more broadly on the role that skies play in painting. The eminent painter and theorist Joshua Reynolds, according to Constable, had said about old-master paintings that "*even their skies seem to sympathize with the Subject.*" The sky, that is, responds to the human dramas unfolding below them. But Constable pushes this relationship between sky and landscape further. "It will be difficult to name a class of Landscape, in which the sky is not the *'key note,'* the *standard of 'Scale,'* and the chief *'Organ of sentiment.'*" Here, Constable suggests that—in landscape at least—the sky is the most expressive element of a painting, the origin of its sense of reality and emotional charge. "The sky is the *'source of light'* in nature—and governs every thing," he wrote. Far from merely serving as a blank backdrop to the landscape below, it animates the landscape and the everyday life that unfolds within it.

Constable lived during a period of profound transformation in theories of climate and meteorology. Meteorological thinkers shared his sense that the world was shaped by the movements of air, moisture, and heat in the atmosphere. It is not surprising, then, that Constable's cloud studies have long been probed—sometimes by meteorologists themselves—for evidence of the artist's scientific knowledge or empirical accuracy. The German art historian Kurt Badt, in his book *John Constable's Clouds* (1950), in fact argued that the painter's precise naturalism was directly influenced by the scientific thinking of the day. In 1802 the Quaker chemist Luke Howard proposed a new system for classifying clouds. First published the following year, this system remains in use today. In Howard's work, the different cloud shapes, or "modifications," as he termed them, found descriptions and names (cumulus, cirrus, stratus, nimbus), much in the way plant or animal species were separated out into classes and types (fig. 11). A striking diagrammatic drawing by Constable's peer William Mulready, from 1840, certainly implies that other artists in the early nineteenth century were looking to Howard (fig. 12). This new way of seeing, according to Badt, must have also been the source of Constable's interest in clouds. The artist owned and annotated an edition of Thomas Forster's *Researches about Atmospheric Phaenomena* that included an overview of Howard's classifications as well as landscape aquatints depicting numbered "specimens" of clouds (figs. 13, 14), though it is not clear when the artist first bought or read Forster's book. Yet in trying to pin down when and how Constable might have encountered these scientific texts and images, we might also be assuming that the artist needed to know about the scientific innovations of his day to pursue his own explorations.

Constable himself saw art as a kind of naturalist inquiry. He believed, as he claimed in a series of lectures delivered near the end of his life, that "painting is a science, and should be pursued as a branch of natural philosophy, of which pictures are but the experiments." He had hoped to assemble a public lecture about his knowledge of trees and clouds, which he kept scattered "on scraps and bits of paper," but did not get around to it. Still, this thinking took place in the medium

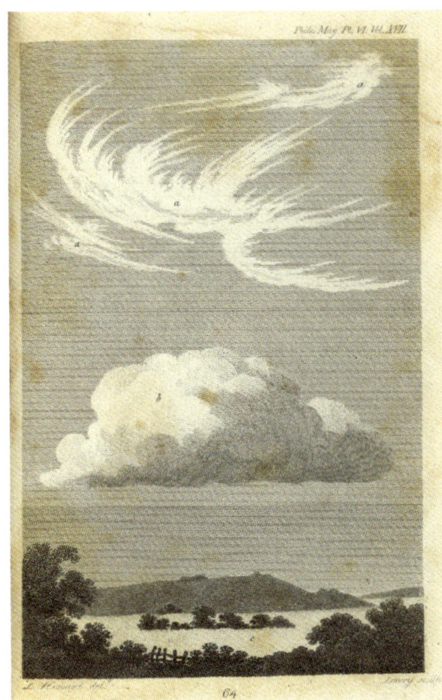

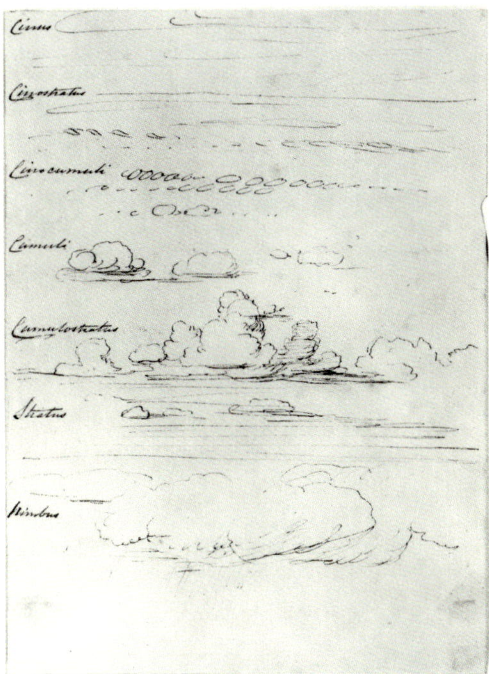

FIG. 11 Wilson Lowry (English, 1762–1824) after Luke Howard (English, 1772–1864), illustration of cirrus, cumulus, and stratus clouds (from "On the Modifications of Clouds, and on the Principles of Their Production, Suspension, and Destruction; Being the Substance of an Essay Read Before the Askesian Society in the Session, 1802–3," *Philosophical Magazine* 16 [1803]), engraving, 6⅞ × 4⅛ in. (17 × 10.6 cm). Yale University, Beinecke Library of Rare Books and Manuscripts

FIG. 12 William Mulready (English, 1786–1863), *Diagrammatic Illustration of Luke Howard's Classification of Clouds*, 1840, pen on paper, 5⅞ × 4¼ in. (14.9 × 10.8 cm). Whitworth Art Gallery, University of Manchester

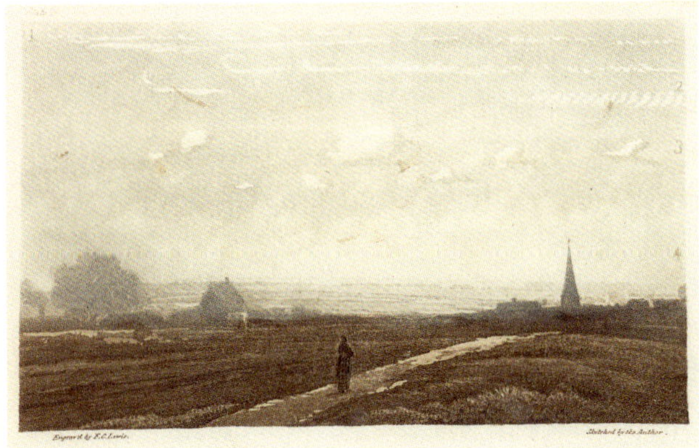

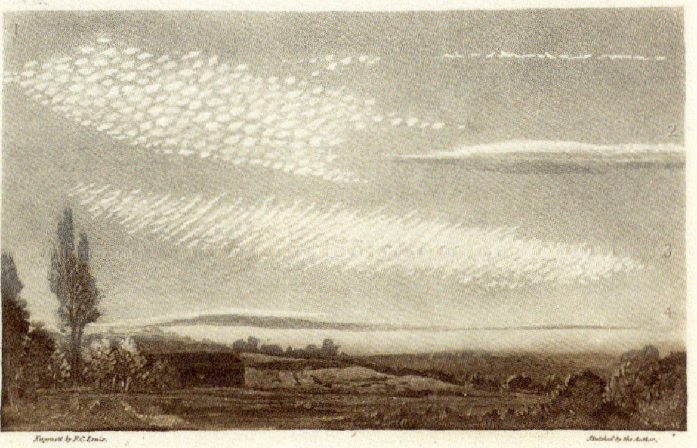

FIGS. 13, 14 Frederick Christian Lewis (English, 1779–1856) after Thomas Forster (English, 1789–1860), illustrations of clouds (from *Researches about Atmospheric Phaenomena*, 2nd ed. [1815]), aquatint, each 4½ × 6⅝ in. (10.5 × 16.9 cm). Yale Center for British Art, Rare Books and Manuscripts

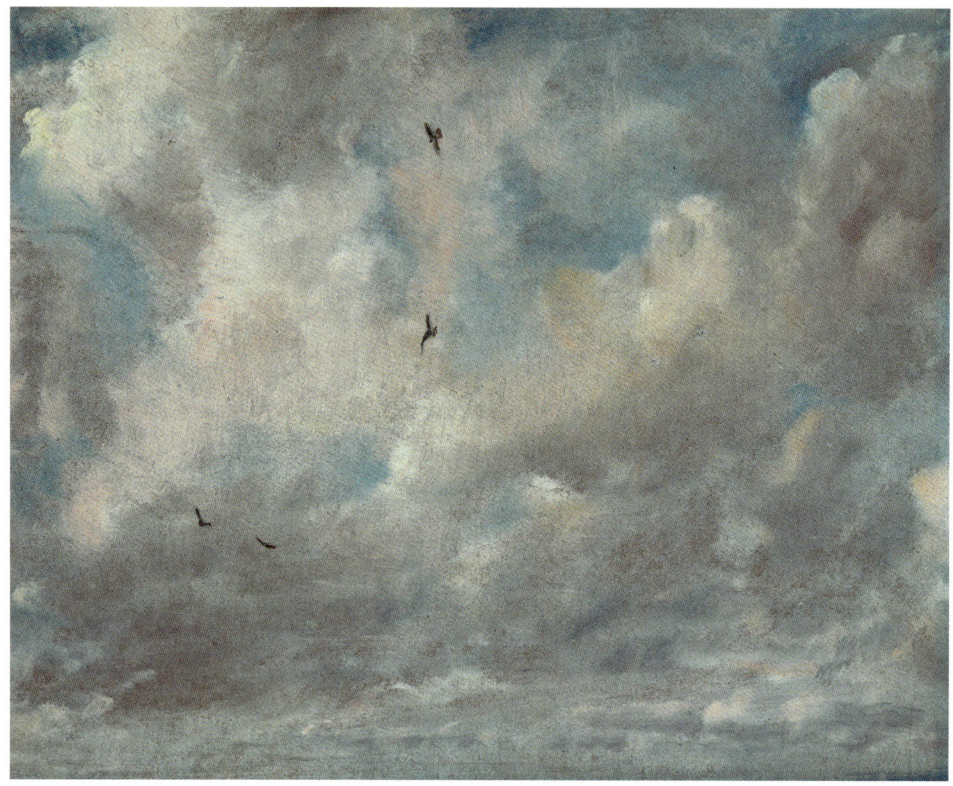

FIG. 15 John Constable, *Cloud Study*, 1821, oil on paper, mounted on board, 9¾ × 11⅞ in. (24.8 × 30.2 cm)

of paint. Some of the realism of the cloud studies—rather than, say, their seemingly abstract quality—has been obscured due to their conversion from sketches into "pictures." We encounter them now as if they were finished paintings, framed and hung on the wall. Their fragile paper supports have been mounted to boards and canvases, stabilized as hefty art objects. In this form they are arresting, but they were never intended to be seen this way. The studies were, perhaps, more like the "scraps and bits of paper" on which Constable made his notes—"little, nameless, unremembered . . . acts," to return to Wordsworth's words, stored up for his own use or to share with his friends and associates. As thin bits of paint on paper, they would look more kindred with the studies of clouds, animals, and plants made by fellow naturalists. Remedying the fragility of their paper origins also means losing something of their relationship to process and experiment.

We might look at these oil sketches now with a slight uneasiness. Constable's seemingly untroubled regard for shifting patterns of light and cloud, the calm notation of everyday wind and rain, feels distant from our present, anxious moment of ecological crisis. In some sketches, like his study *Somerset House Terrace from Waterloo Bridge* (plate 36), with its turgid and smoky sky, he seems to be registering the ways the forces of modernity were changing the climate around it; as Tim Barringer notes in his essay, this would become the theme of his *The Opening of Waterloo Bridge* (see p. 26, fig. 16). We might also question how much Constable—son of a landowner and barge operator who transported coal along the River Stour—would have understood himself to be a part of those forces. Yet we might also see how his cloud studies are concerned with the experience of inhabiting a vulnerable body in a world of change. As Howard wrote, "The sky too belongs to the landscape"; it is the "ocean of air in which we live and move." Look at the cloud study, thought to have been made sometime in 1821, that captures four birds as they fly through the air (fig. 15). They drift in accord with a wind that we cannot, ourselves, sense. They represent the experience of being moved by larger forces, of acting and being acted upon. This sense of vulnerability and exposure—both pleasurable and otherwise—is perhaps one of the lessons that these "scraps and bits of paper" still have to teach us.

NOTES

MR. CONSTABLE'S ENGLISH LANDSCAPE

p. 9 **"chiar'oscuro of nature":** John Constable, *Various Subjects of Landscape, Characteristic of English Scenery, from Pictures Painted by John Constable, R. A.* (*English Landscape*), mezzotints engraved by David Lucas, 2nd ed. (London, 1833), title page (hereafter cited as *English Landscape*). See Andrew Wilton, *Constable's "English Landscape Scenery"* (London: British Museum Publications, 1979), 21.

"This spot saw the day-spring": See "Additional Verses" under Constable, letterpress accompanying *East Bergholt, Sussex* (from *English Landscape*, 2nd ed. [1833]), in *John Constable's Discourses*, ed. R. B. Beckett (Ipswich, UK: Suffolk Records Society, 1970), 14. The Latin text is from *On the Praise of Divine Wisdom*, by the twelfth-century theologian Alexander Neckam. See Richard Humphreys, *John Constable: The Leaping Horse* (London: Royal Academy of Arts, 2018), 53.

p. 14 **Cranch introduced Constable to the major texts:** James Hamilton, *John Constable: A Portrait* (London: Weidenfeld and Nicolson, 2022), 54.

p. 15 **"my *old men*":** John Constable to George Constable, December 20, 1833, in *John Constable's Correspondence*, ed. Beckett, vol. 5, *Various Friends, with Charles Boner and the Artist's Children* (Ipswich, UK: Suffolk Records Society, 1967), 16 (hereafter cited as *JCC*). See also Mark Evans, "Collector: 'The Interesting and Valuable Collection formed by the Late John Constable, Esq. R. A.,'" in *John Constable: The Making of a Master*, exh. cat. (London: Victoria and Albert Museum, 2014), 87.

p. 17 **Constable admired the "freshness and dewy light":** Beckett, *John Constable's Discourses*, 61.

Rubens, Constable added, "delighted in phenomena": Beckett, *John Constable's Discourses*, 61.

At this time, he wrote a letter to Dunthorne: Constable to John Dunthorne, May 29, 1802, in *JCC*, ed. Beckett, vol. 2, *Early Friends and Maria Bicknell (Mrs. Constable)* (1964), 32.

p. 19 **He proclaimed himself to be "determined to finish":** Constable to Dunthorne, February 22, 1814, in *JCC*, ed. Beckett, vol. 1, *The Family at East Bergholt, 1807–1837* (1962), 101.

he had been "long occupied in painting Landscapes from nature": Entry for November 5, 1814, *The Diary of Joseph Farington*, ed. Kathryn Cave, vol. 13, *January 1814 – December 1815* (New Haven, CT: Yale University Press, 1984), 4603.

p. 22 **Some elements of the composition appear in a vertical oil sketch:** Leslie Parris and Ian Fleming-Williams, "The London Years: Early Set Pieces," in *Constable*, exh. cat. (London: Tate Gallery, 1991), 198.

p. 24 **Rooted in memory, it is a loving assemblage:** Franklin Kelly, "Stratford Mill," in *Constable: The Great Landscapes*, exh. cat., ed. Anne Lyles (London: Tate Publishing, 2006), 136–39.

"But I should paint my own places best": Constable to Rev. John Fisher, October 23, 1821, in *JCC*, ed. Beckett, vol. 6, *The Fishers* (1968), 78.

p. 25 **As he wrote to Fisher, he could "above all see nature":** Constable to Rev. Fisher, November 28, 1826, in *JCC*, 6:228.

the "chief '*Organ of sentiment*'": Constable to Rev. Fisher, 23 October 1821, in *JCC*, 6:77.

The ostensible subject is one of metropolitan and imperial triumph: Lyles, "The Opening of Waterloo Bridge," in *The Great Landscapes*, 184–89.

p. 26 **By February 1832 Constable could write, "I am dashing away":** Constable to David Lucas, February 28, 1832, in *JCC*, ed. Beckett, vol. 4, *Patrons, Dealers, and Fellow Artists* (1966), 368.

Constable "had indulged in the vagaries of the palette knife": Charles Robert Leslie, *Memoirs of the Life of John Constable*, 2nd ed. (London, 1845), 226.

Constable called it "my Harlequin's Jacket": Constable to Leslie, March 3, 1832, in *JCC*, ed. Beckett, vol. 3, *The Correspondence with C. R. Leslie, R. A.* (1965), 63.

p. 27 **"A sea piece by Turner was next to it":** Walter Thornbury, *The Life of J. M. W. Turner, R. A.* (London, 1862), 2:187. See also Michael Rosenthal, "Turner Fires a Gun," in *Art on the Line: The Royal Academy Exhibitions at Somerset House, 1780–1836*, ed. David H. Solkin (New Haven, CT: Yale University Press, 2001), 145–56.

The aging painter foresaw a dystopian future: Constable to Leslie, late October 1831, in *JCC*, 3:49.

p. 28 **"Hourly do I feel the loss":** Constable to Golding Constable, December 19, 1928, in *JCC*, 1:252, quoted in Kelly, "Hadleigh Castle," in *The Great Landscapes*, 174.

p. 29 **"It has been delayed until I am solitary":** Leslie, *Memoirs*, 186.

p. 30 **"It is mighty fine—though it looks as if all the chimney sweepers":** Constable to Lucas, February 26, 1830, in *JCC*, 4:325.

p. 31 **it offered the "fullest impression":** Leslie, *Memoirs*, 259.

The painter revered the "venerable grandeur": Constable, letterpress accompanying *Stoke by Nayland, Suffolk* (from *English Landscape*, 2nd ed. [1833]), in Beckett, *John Constable's Discourses*, 23.

p. 32 **Sarum once witnessed the "establishment of the feudal system":** Constable, letterpress accompanying *Old Sarum*, in Beckett, *John Constable's Discourses*, 25.

p. 34 **The curator of the Museum of Modern Art's 1956 exhibition:** Andrew Carnduff Ritchie, "John Constable: 1776–1837," in *Masters of British Painting, 1800–1950*, exh. cat. (New York: Museum of Modern Art, 1956), 24.

EARLY PAINTINGS AND OIL SKETCHES

p. 37 **Constable insisted on the value of "laborious studies":** Constable to John Dunthorne, May 29, 1802, in *JCC*, 2:32.

"You know I have succeeded most with my native scenes": Constable to Maria Bicknell, May 27, 1812, in *JCC*, 2:70.

p. 38 **Wilson's student William Hodges:** Rosenthal, "The Nature of British Landscape Painting, c. 1770–1830," in *Turner and Constable: Sketching from Nature*, exh. cat., ed. Steven Parissien (London: Tate, 2013), 13.
Constable found it "bleak": Constable to Dunthorne, February 22, 1814, in *JCC*, 1:101.

LATER PAINTINGS AND OIL SKETCHES

p. 51 **"I do not consider myself at work":** Constable to Rev. Fisher, October 23, 1821, in *JCC*, 6:76.
When Constable heard from Reverend Fisher . . . he responded gloomily: Rev. Fisher to Constable, September [1825], and Constable to Rev. Fisher, November 12, 1825, in *JCC*, 6:206–7.

DRAWINGS AND WATERCOLORS

p. 75 **Smith also recommended penetrating "into the inmost recesses":** John Thomas Smith, *Remarks on Rural Scenery* (London, 1797), 12.
Constable found himself "quite alone among the Oaks": Constable to Dunthorne, July 1800, in *JCC*, 2:25.

PRINTS

p. 95 **the walls of the artist's bedroom "were covered with engravings":** Leslie, *Autobiographical Recollections*, ed. Tom Taylor (London, 1860), 1:158, quoted in Evans, "*Collector*," 81.
the "just observation of natural scenery in its various aspects": Constable, letterpress introduction (from *English Landscape*), facsimile reproduced in Wilton, *Constable's "English Landscape Scenery,"* 24.

p. 96 **Constable bridled against Turner's "liber stupidorum":** Constable to Lucas, March 12, 1831, in *JCC*, 4:344–5. See Gillian Forrester, *Turner's "Drawing Book": The Liber Studiorum*, exh. cat. (London: Tate, 1996).
Looking at a proof of *A Summerland*: Constable to Lucas, February 26, 1830, in *JCC*, 4:325.
The final version of each image evolved slowly: Parris and Fleming-Williams, "The London Years: The 1830s," in *Constable*, 367–8.
"This plate may perhaps give some idea": Constable, letterpress accompanying *Spring* (from *English Landscape*), text reproduced in Wilton, *Constable's English Landscape Scenery*, 32.
chiaroscuro was the "medium by which the grand and varied aspects": Constable, 1835 Prospectus for *English Landscape*, in Beckett, *John Constable's Discourses*, 11.

"LITTLE, NAMELESS, UNREMEMBERED": CONSTABLE'S CLOUDS

p. 107 **Alongside paintings of "grand subjects":** *A Catalogue of the Valuable Finished Works, Studies and Sketches of John Constable, Esq. R. A.* (London, 1838), quoted in Ian Fleming-Williams and Leslie Parris, *The Discovery of Constable* (London: Hamish Hamilton, 1984), 15.

to find, in William Wordsworth's words, "A motion and a spirit": William Wordsworth, "Lines Composed a Few Miles above Tintern Abbey," in *Selected Poems*, ed. Stephen Gill (New York: Penguin, 2004), 61.

p. 108 **a way to "see into the life of things":** Wordsworth, "Tintern Abbey," 61. See Karl Kroeber, *Romantic Landscape Vision: Constable and Wordsworth* (Madison: University of Wisconsin Press, 1975).

Reporting on the sale of Constable's effects: "Our Weekly Gossip," *Athenaeum*, May 5, 1838, 326.

p. 109 **Sketching outdoors required artists:** Ann Bermingham, "Reading Constable," *Art History* 10, no. 1 (1987): 39–42.

p. 110 **Here, what the artist called the "chiaro'scuro of nature":** John Constable, *Various Subjects of Landscape, Characteristic of English Scenery* (*English Landscape*), mezzotints engraved by David Lucas, 2nd ed. (London, 1833), title page (hereafter *English Landscape*).

As Constable put it, Claude "lived in the fields all day": Constable, "Lectures on Landscape" (1836), in *John Constable's Discourses*, ed. R. B. Beckett (Ipswich, UK: Suffolk Records Society: 1970), 53.

British landscape painters before him: Anne Lyles, "'That Immense Canopy': Studies of Sky and Cloud by British Artists, c. 1770–1860," in *Constable's Clouds: Paintings and Cloud Studies by John Constable*, exh. cat., ed. Edward Morris (Edinburgh: National Galleries of Scotland, 2000), 135–50.

p. 111 **they might be understood to form a "natural history . . . of the skies":** Constable, letterpress accompanying *Spring* (from *English Landscape*, 2nd ed. [1833]), in *John Constable's Discourses*, 14.

p. 112 **As the artist's contemporary William Hazlitt wrote about painting:** [William Hazlitt], "On the Pleasure of Painting," *London Magazine*, December 1820, 598.

p. 113 **he experimented with laminating different paper grounds together:** Sarah Cove, "Constable's Oil Painting Materials and Techniques," in Leslie Parris and Ian Fleming-Williams, *Constable*, exh. cat. (London: Tate Gallery, 1991), 498–500; Peter Bower, "Catching the Sky: The Papers and Boards Used by John Constable for His Studies of Sky and Cloud," in *Constable's Skies*, exh. cat., ed. Frederic Bancroft (New York: Salander-O'Reilly Galleries, 2004), 153–79.

Constable mixed his paints using pre-ground pigments from color suppliers: Cove, "Constable's Oil Painting Materials and Techniques," 504–7, 514–15.

He wanted his work to body forth: Constable to Charles Robert Leslie, March 1833, in *John Constable's Correspondence*, ed. Beckett, vol. 3, *The Correspondence with C. R. Leslie, R. A.* (Ipswich, UK: Suffolk Record Society, 1965), 96 (hereafter *JCC*).

p. 115 **The meteorologist John E. Thornes:** John E. Thornes, *John Constable's Skies* (Birmingham, UK: University of Birmingham Press, 1999), 59.

The eminent painter and theorist Joshua Reynolds: Constable to Rev. John Fisher, October 23, 1821, in *JCC*, vol. 6, *The Fishers* (1968), 76.

"It will be difficult to name a class of Landscape": Constable to Rev. Fisher, October 23, 1821, in *JCC*, 6:77

p. 116 **"The sky is the *'source of light'* in nature"**: Constable to Rev. Fisher, October 23, 1821, in *JCC*, 6:77.

Meteorological thinkers shared his sense that the world: Nicholas Robbins, "John Constable, Luke Howard, and the Aesthetics of Climate," *Art Bulletin* 103, no. 2 (2021): 50–76.

It is not surprising, then, that Constable's cloud studies: See, for example, L. C. W. Bonacina, "John Constable's Centenary: His Position as a Painter of Weather," *Quarterly Journal of the Royal Meteorological Society* 63, no. 272 (October 1937): 483–90; Thornes, *John Constable's Skies*.

The German art historian Kurt Badt: Kurt Badt, *John Constable's Clouds* (London: Routledge & Kegan Paul, 1950).

First published the following year: These were first published in a series of articles in *The Philosophical Magazine* and collected in Luke Howard, *On the Modifications of Clouds* (London, 1803).

"painting is a science": Constable, "Lectures on Landscape" (1836), in *John Constable's Discourses*, 69.

He had hoped to assemble a public lecture: Constable to George Constable, December 12, 1836, quoted in Beckett, "Lectures on Landscape: Introductory Note," in *John Constable's Discourses*, 35.

p. 118 **The studies were, perhaps, more like the "scraps and bits of paper"**: Wordsworth, "Tintern Abbey," 61. See Bower, "Catching the Sky," 153.

Constable's seemingly untroubled regard for shifting patterns: Gillen D'Arcy Wood, "Constable, Clouds, Climate Change," *Wordsworth Circle* 38, nos. 1–2 (2007): 25–33.

p. 119 **As Howard wrote, "the sky too belongs to the landscape"**: Luke Howard, *Seven Lectures on Meteorology*, 2nd ed. (London, 1843), 2.

FOR FURTHER READING

Mark Evans; with Stephen Calloway and Susan Owens, *John Constable: The Making of a Master* (London: V & A Publishing, 2014).

Gillian Forrester, *John Constable* (London: Tate Publishing, 2024).

Matthew Hargraves and Anne Lyles, *Late Constable* (London: Royal Academy of Arts, 2021).

James Hamilton, *John Constable, A Portrait* (London: Pegasus, 2022).

William Kentridge and Aimee Ng, *Constable's White Horse* (New York: Frick Collection, 2020).

Anne Lyles, ed., *Constable: The Great Landscapes* (London: Tate Publishing, 2006).

Nicola Moorby, *Turner and Constable: Art, Life, Landscape* (New Haven, CT: Yale University Press, 2025).

Christine Riding and Mary McMahon, *Discover Constable & The Hay Wain* (London: National Gallery, 2024).

INDEX

Note: Illustrations are indicated by page numbers in *italics*. Accession numbers in parentheses denote works held by the Yale Center for British Art.